www.wadsworth.com

www.wadsworth.com is the World Wide Web site for Wadsworth and is your direct source to dozens of online resources.

At *www.wadsworth.com* you can find out about supplements, demonstration software, and student resources. You can also send email to many of our authors and preview new publications and exciting new technologies.

www.wadsworth.com
Changing the way the world learns®

CALIFORNIA POLITICS AND GOVERNMENT

A Practical Approach

Eighth Edition

Larry N. Gerston
San Jose State University

Terry Christensen
San Jose State University

THOMSON
WADSWORTH

Australia • Canada • Mexico • Singapore • Spain
United Kingdom • United States

THOMSON
WADSWORTH

Publisher, Political Science: Clark Baxter
Executive Editor, Political Science: David Tatom
Senior Developmental Editor: Stacey Sims
Assistant Editor: Rebecca Green
Technology Project Manager: Michelle Vardeman
Marketing Manager: Janise Fry
Advertising Project Manager: Kelly McAllister
Project Manager, Editorial Production: Paul Wells
Art Director: Maria Epes

Printed in Canada
1 2 3 4 5 6 7 09 08 07 06 05

Library of Congress Control Number: 2004113384

ISBN 0-534-63081-2

Print/Media Buyer: Lisa Claudeanos
Permissions Editor: Stephanie Lee
Production Service: G&S Book Services
Copy Editor: Laurie Baker
Illustrator: G&S Book Services
Cover Designer: Sue Hart
Cover Image: Getty Images/Doug Menuez
Compositor: G&S Book Services
Text and Cover Printer: Webcom

Thomson Higher Education
10 Davis Drive
Belmont, CA 94002-3098
USA

Asia (including India)
Thomson Learning
5 Shenton Way
#01-01 UIC Building
Singapore 068808

Australia/New Zealand
Thomson Learning Australia
102 Dodds Street
Southbank, Victoria 3006
Australia

Canada
Thomson Nelson
1120 Birchmount Road
Toronto, Ontario M1K 5G4
Canada

UK/Europe/Middle East/Africa
Thomson Learning
High Holborn House
50-51 Bedford Row
London WC1R 4LR

Latin America
Thomson Learning
Seneca, 53
Colonia Polanco
11560 Mexico
D.F. Mexico

Spain (including Portugal)
Thomson Paraninfo
Calle Magallanes, 25
28015 Madrid, Spain

To
the futures of
Adam David, Lee Daniel, and
Rachel Sarah Gerston

and

the memories of
Anna and Teter Christensen and
Tillie and Chester Welliever

CONTENTS

PREFACE

California Politics and Government introduces observers, participants, and students to the state's politics. Using down-to-earth, readable language and examples, we have attempted to cover the topic in a way that balances the basics of state politics and government with analysis, color, and brevity. As with earlier editions, we emphasize California's political institutions and processes. The state's historical evolution dominates our first chapter. Succeeding chapters on political institutions include their historical development as well as their current operations. Cultural diversity is another theme that runs through every chapter. We have included the nuts and bolts of the political process and institutions, along with frequent references to the people, groups, and issues that move them. Most of all, we have tried to make sense out of the maze of contradictions known as California.

In earlier editions of this book, we noted the rapidity of change in California and its politics. Yet, the jolts from past gyrations seem minimal, compared to the revolution wrought by the recall of Governor Gray Davis in 2003. Not only did that historical event repudiate the outcome of an election that took place just months before, it also provided a platform for anger about some of the state's unresolved political issues such as the electricity shortage, a budget deficit almost incomprehensible in size, and a recession that threatened virtually every element of the state. Because of the recall's impact on so many aspects of California, we have included discussion about this revolution in several chapters, rather than merely attaching an appendix in the most convenient section.

As the state changes, so must *California Politics and Government.* Thus, in the state-federal relations chapter, we focus more attention on the increasingly important–and often testy–relationship between California and the national government, particularly with respect to immigration and homeland security. Additionally, in other chapters, we focus on the emergence of new or strengthened players, such as the Indian gaming interests and the state prison guards' union, as well as the continued emergence of Latinos, the state's largest ethnic minority, as a growing force on the state's political scene. None was recognized for having much clout as recently as a few years ago; today they carry great weight.

For those who want information beyond what is offered in the book we have also updated "Learn More on the World Wide Web" and "Learn More at the Library." These tools give the reader additional online sources and library materials on some of the key topics discussed in the chapters. As in previous editions, key terms, institutions, and events are printed in bold throughout the book. These terms are briefly defined in the glossary at the back of our book to provide a quick reference source for students.

Many friends and colleagues helped us develop and produce this book. Peter Tessier provided timely and intrepid research assistance. Staff members in the governor's office, the legislature, the courts, and other government departments helped us in our search for the most current data. We would especially like to thank the following reviewers whose comments contributed to this revision: Amber Casolari, Glendale Community College; Tod Kunioka, California State University, Los Angeles; Sunday P. Obazuaye, Cerritos College; and Mark Summa, California State University, Fresno. We continue to learn from our students who, with each edition, challenge us to provide essential information and analysis in the most understandable fashion. And we are indebted to our many friends in politics, journalism, and academia for their input.

We are grateful to the production staff at Wadsworth who worked on an unusually tight schedule. They include David Tatom, executive editor; Stacey Sims, developmental editor; Paul Wells, production project manager; and Janise Fry, marketing manager. Thanks also to Maria Epes, art director, and Sue Hart for her excellent cover design. To these and many others, we offer our deepest thanks.

Larry N. Gerston
Terry Christensen
December 31, 2004

ABOUT THE AUTHORS

Larry N. Gerston, professor of political science at San Jose State University, attempts to blend politics and theory whenever possible, viewing both as key components of the political process. He has worked for a Los Angeles County supervisor and a California assembly member. Professor Gerston has written *Making Public Policy: From Conflict to Resolution* (1983), *American Government: Politics, Process, and Policies* (1993), *Public Policy Making: Process and Principles* (1997), and *Public Policymaking in a Democratic Society: A Guide to Civic Engagement* (2002). He has co-authored *Recall! California's Political Earthquake* (2004) and *Politics in the Golden State* (1984, 1988) with Terry Christensen and *The Deregulated Society* (1988) with Cynthia Fraleigh and Robert Schwab. Professor Gerston writes a monthly column on politics for *San Jose Magazine* and has served since 1980 as the political analyst for television station NBC11 in San Jose. Between elections and other political adventures, he enjoys his wife, Elisa, and their three children, Adam, Lee, and Rachel.

Terry Christensen, professor of political science at San Jose State University, teaches and writes on California state and local politics and urban planning. He has authored *Neighborhood Survival* (1979), a book about urban renewal in London; *Movers and Shakers* (1982, with Philip J. Trounstine), a study of community power; *Reel Politics* (1987), an analysis of American political movies; *Local Politics: Governing at the Grassroots* (1995); and *Recall! California's Political Earthquake* (2004, with Larry N. Gerston). He's currently at work on new editions of *Reel Politics* and *Local Politics.* A longtime political activist, Christensen has worked with a wide variety of community organizations and political campaigns and has served as a delegate to the South Bay AFL-CIO Labor Council and on the Executive Board of the Commonwealth Club/Silicon Valley. As his history may suggest, he advocates learning by participant observation, and he helped develop San Jose State's extensive internship program. He was selected San Jose State University's Outstanding Professor for 1997–1998.

CHAPTER 1

CALIFORNIA'S PEOPLE, ECONOMY, AND POLITICS: YESTERDAY, TODAY, AND TOMORROW

Like so much else about California, our state's politics appear to change constantly, unpredictably, and even inexplicably. Politicians seem to rise and fall more because of their personalities and campaign treasuries than because of their policies. The governor and the legislature appear to be competing with one another rather than solving our problems. Decisions about sometimes major and sometimes trivial issues are put to the voters only to see the courts overturn their decisions. Nothing illustrates this better than the recall election of 2003 when the voters removed Governor Gray Davis from office less than a year after re-electing him and then replaced him with political novice and movie star Arnold Schwarzenegger.

Californians and the rest of the world are amazed and mystified that such things can happen in a state that is so rich, powerful, and seemingly sophisticated. But however unpredictable or volatile California politics may seem, it is serious business that affects us all, and it can be understood by examining the history and present characteristics of our state–especially its changing population and economy. Wave after wave of immigrants has made California a diverse, multicultural society, while new technologies repeatedly transform the state's economy. The resulting disparate ethnic and economic interests compete for the benefits and protections conferred by government and thus shape the state's politics. But to understand California today–and tomorrow–we need to know a little about its past and about the development of these competing interests.

COLONIZATION, REBELLION, AND STATEHOOD

The first Californians were probably immigrants like the rest of us. Archaeologists believe that the ancestors of American Indians crossed over from Asia to Alaska thousands of years ago and then headed south.

Europeans began exploring the California coast in the 1500s, but colonization didn't begin until 1769, when the Spanish established a string of missions and military outposts. About 300,000 Native Americans were living mostly near the coast at that time.

These native Californians were brought to the missions as Catholic converts and workers, but European diseases and the destruction of the native culture reduced their numbers to about 100,000 by 1849. Disease and massacres wiped out entire tribes, and the Indian population continued to diminish throughout the nineteenth century. Today, less than 1 percent of California's population is Native American. Many of them feel deeply alienated from a society that has overwhelmed their peoples, cultures, and traditions.

Apart from building missions, the Spaniards did little to develop their faraway possession, and little changed when Mexico, which included California within its boundaries, declared its independence from Spain in 1822. A few thousand Mexicans quietly raised cattle on vast ranches and continued to build the province's small towns around their central plazas.

Meanwhile, expansionist interests in the United States cast covetous eyes on California's rich lands and access to the Pacific Ocean. When Mexico and the United States went to war over Texas in 1846, recent Yankee immigrants to California seized the moment and declared independence from Mexico. After the U.S. victory in Texas, Mexico surrendered its claim to lands extending from Texas to California. By this time, foreigners already outnumbered Californians of Spanish ancestry 9,000 to 7,500.

In 1848, gold was discovered, and the '49ers who arrived the next year or soon after brought the nonnative population to 264,000 by 1852. Many immigrants came directly from Europe. The first Chinese people also arrived to work in the mines, which yielded more than a billion dollars' worth of gold in 5 years.

The surge in population and commerce moved the new Californians to political action. By 1849 they had drafted a constitution, mostly copied from those of existing states, and requested statehood, which the U.S. Congress was only too glad to grant. The organization of the new state was remarkably similar to what we have today. The 48 delegates to the constitutional convention (only seven of whom were native-born Californians) set up a two-house legislature, a supreme court, and an executive branch consisting of a governor, lieutenant governor, controller, attorney general, and superintendent of public instruction. A bill of rights was also included in the constitution, but only white males were allowed to vote. The rights of women and racial minorities were ignored, and in addition to being denied the right to vote, California's Chinese, African American, and Native American residents were soon prohibited by law from owning land, testifying in court, or attending public schools.

The voters approved the constitution in 1849, and San Jose became the first state capitol. The city bought an adobe hotel to serve as a temporary capital, and newly elected legislators crowded into town. With housing in short supply, many had to lodge in tents, and the primitive living conditions were exacerbated by heavy rain and flooding. They nevertheless became known as "the legislature of a thousand drinks." The state capitol soon moved on to Vallejo and Benicia, finally settling in 1854 in Sacramento—closer to the gold fields.

As the gold rush ended, a land rush began. Unlike the land in other states, where small homesteads predominated, much of California's land had been divided into huge tracts by Spanish and Mexican land grants. As early as 1870, a few hundred men owned most of the farmland. Their ranches were the forerunners of contemporary agribusiness corporations, and as the mainstay of the state's economy, they exercised even more clout than their modern successors.

In less than 50 years, California had belonged to three different nations. During the same period, its economy had changed dramatically as hundreds of thousands of immigrants from all over the world came to claim their share of the "Golden State." The pattern of a rapidly evolving, multicultural polity had been set.

RAILROADS, MACHINES, AND REFORM

Technology wrought the next transformation in the form of railroads. In 1861 Sacramento merchants Charles Crocker, Mark Hopkins, Collis Huntington, and Leland Stanford founded the railroad that would become the **Southern Pacific.** Then they persuaded Congress to provide millions of dollars in land grants and loan subsidies for a railroad to link California with the eastern United States, thus greatly expanding the market for California products. Leland Stanford, then governor, used his influence to provide state assistance. Cities and counties also contributed, under the threat of being bypassed by the railroad. To obtain workers at cheap rates, the railroad builders imported 15,000 Chinese laborers.

When the transcontinental track was completed in 1869, the Southern Pacific expanded its system throughout the state by building new lines and buying up existing ones. The railroad crushed competitors by cutting its shipping charges, and by the 1880s it had become the state's dominant transportation company as well as its largest private landowner, owning 11 percent of the entire state. With its business agents doubling as political representatives in almost every California city and county, the Southern Pacific soon developed a formidable political machine. "The Octopus," as novelist Frank Norris called the railroad, worked through both the Republican and Democratic political parties to place allies in state and local offices. Once there, they were obliged to protect the interests of the

Southern Pacific if they wanted to continue in office. County tax assessors who were supported by the machine set favorable tax rates for the railroad, while the machine-controlled legislature ensured a hands-off policy by state government.

THE WORKINGMEN'S PARTY

People in small towns and rural areas who were unwilling to support the machine lost jobs, business, and other benefits. Some moved to cities, especially San Francisco, where manufacturing jobs were increasingly available. Many of the Chinese workers who were brought to California to build the railroad also sought work in the cities when it was completed. However, when jobs became scarce in the 1870s because of a depression, they faced hostile treatment from earlier immigrants. Led by Denis Kearney, Irish immigrants became the core of the **Workingmen's party,** a political organization that blamed the railroad and the Chinese for their economic difficulties.

Small farmers opposed to the railroad united through the Grange movement. In 1879 the Grangers and the Workingmen's party called California's second constitutional convention in hopes of breaking the power of the railroad. The new constitution that they created mandated regulation of railroads, utilities, banks, and other corporations. An elected state Board of Equalization was set up to ensure the fairness of local tax assessments on railroads and their friends, as well as their enemies. The new constitution also prohibited the Chinese from owning land, voting, or working for state or local government.

The railroad soon reclaimed power, however, gaining control of the agencies created to regulate it and, spurred on by the discovery of oil in the Los Angeles area, pushing growth in Southern California. Nonetheless, the efforts made during this period to regulate big business and control racial tensions became recurring themes in California life and politics, and much of the Constitution of 1879 remains intact today.

THE PROGRESSIVES

The growth fostered by the railroad eventually produced a new middle class. The economy grew more urban and more diverse, encompassing merchants, doctors, lawyers, teachers, and skilled workers who were not dependent on the railroad. They objected to the corrupt practices and favoritism of the railroad's political machine, which they thought was holding back the economic development of their communities. Instead, the new middle class demanded honesty and competence, which they called "good government." In 1907 a number of these crusaders established the Lincoln-Roosevelt League, a reform group within the Republican party, and became part of the national **Progressive** movement. They elected their leader, Hiram Johnson, to the governorship in 1910, and they also captured control of the state legislature.

To break the power of the machine, the Progressives introduced reforms that have shaped California politics to this day. Predictably, they created a new regulatory agency, the Public Utilities Commission (PUC), for the railroads and utilities; most of their reforms, however, were aimed at weakening the political parties as tools of bosses and machines. Instead of party bosses handpicking candidates at party conventions, the voters were given the power to select their party's nominees for office in **primary elections. Cross-filing** further diluted party power by allowing candidates to file for and win the nominations of more than one political party. The Progressives made city and county elections **nonpartisan** by removing party labels from the ballot altogether. They also created a **civil service** system to select state employees on the basis of their qualifications rather than their political connections.

Finally, the Progressives introduced **direct democracy,** which allowed the voters to amend the constitution and create laws through initiatives and referenda and to recall, or remove, elected officials before their term expired. Supporters of an initiative, referendum, or recall must circulate petitions and collect a specified number of signatures of registered voters before it becomes a ballot measure or proposition.

Like the Workingmen's party before them, the Progressives were concerned about immigration. Antagonism toward recently arrived Japanese immigrants (72,000 by 1910) led the Progressives to ban land ownership by aliens and to support the National Immigration Act of 1924, which effectively halted Japanese immigration. More-positive changes under the Progressives included women gaining the right to vote, child labor and workers' compensation laws, and conservation programs to protect natural resources.

The railroad's political machine eventually died, although California's increasingly diverse economy probably had as much to do with its demise as the Progressive reforms did. The emerging oil, automobile, and trucking industries gave the state important alternative means of transportation and shipping. The reform movement waned in the 1920s, but the Progressive legacy of weak political parties and direct democracy opened up California's politics to its citizens, as well as to individual candidates with strong personalities and powerful interest groups.

THE GREAT DEPRESSION AND WORLD WAR II

California's population grew by more than 2 million in the 1920s (Table 1.1). Most of the newcomers headed for Los Angeles, where employment opportunities in shipping, filmmaking, and manufacturing

TABLE 1.1

CALIFORNIA'S POPULATION GROWTH, SELECTED DECADES, 1850–2004

YEAR	POPULATION	PERCENTAGE OF U.S. POPULATION
1850	93,000	0.4
1900	1,485,000	2.0
1950	10,643,000	7.0
1960	15,863,000	8.8
1970	20,039,000	9.8
1980	23,780,000	10.5
1990	29,733,000	11.7
2000	33,871,648	12.0
2004	36,144,000	12.3

SOURCE: U.S. Census and California Department of Finance.

(clothing, automobiles, and aircraft) abounded. The Great Depression of the 1930s saw an unemployment rate of 33 percent, but over a million people still came to California, including thousands of poor white immigrants from the Midwest Dust Bowl. Many wandered through California's great Central Valley in search of work, displacing Mexicans, who earlier had supplanted the Chinese and Japanese, as the state's farm workers. Racial antagonism ran high, and many Mexicans were arbitrarily sent back to Mexico. Labor unrest reached a crescendo in the early 1930s, as workers on farms, in canneries, and on the docks of San Francisco and Los Angeles fought for higher wages and an 8-hour workday.

The immigrants and union activists of the 1920s and 1930s also changed California politics. Many registered as Democrats, thus challenging the dominant Republicans. The Depression and President Franklin Roosevelt's popular New Deal helped the Democrats become California's majority party in registration, although winning elections proved more difficult. Their biggest boost came from Upton Sinclair, a novelist, a socialist, and the Democratic candidate for governor in 1934. His End Poverty in California (EPIC) movement almost led to an election victory, but the state's conservative establishment spent an unprecedented $10 million attacking and ultimately defeating him. The Democrats finally gained the governorship in 1938, but their candidate, Culbert Olson, was the only Democratic winner between 1894 and 1958.

World War II revived the economic boom; California's radio, electronics, and aircraft industries grew at phenomenal rates. The jobs brought new immigrants, including many African Americans. Although their proportion of the state's population doubled during the 1940s, African Americans were on the periphery of the state's racial conflicts. Meanwhile, suspected of loyalty to their ancestral homeland, 111,000 Japanese Americans were sent to prison camps (officially called "internment" centers) during the war. Mexican Americans, too, were victimized when Anglo sailors and police, identifying them by their "Zoot suit" style of clothing, attacked them in Los Angeles in the "Zoot Suit Riots" of 1943.

While the cities boomed, the Central Valley bloomed, thanks to water projects initiated by the state and federal governments during the 1930s. Dams and canals brought water to the desert and reaffirmed agriculture as a mainstay of California's economy. The defense industries that supplemented California's industrial base during the war became permanent fixtures, with aerospace and electronics adding to their momentum.

Although the voters had chosen a Democratic governor during the Depression, they returned to the Republican fold as the economy revived. Earl Warren, who symbolized a new breed of Republican, was elected governor in 1942, 1946, and 1950, becoming the only individual to win the office three times. Warren used cross-filing to win the nominations of both parties and staked out a relationship with the voters that he claimed was above party politics. A classic example of California's personality-oriented politics, Warren left the state in 1953 to become chief justice of the U.S. Supreme Court.

POSTWAR POLITICS

In 1958, with the Republican party in disarray because of infighting, Californians elected a Democratic governor, Edmund G. "Pat" Brown, and a Democratic majority in the state legislature. To prevent Republicans from taking advantage of cross-filing again, the state's new leaders immediately outlawed that electoral device.

In control of both the governor's office and the legislature for the first time in the twentieth century, Democrats moved aggressively to develop the state's infrastructure. Completion of the massive California Water Project, construction of the state highway network, and organization of the higher education system were among the advances made to accommodate a growing population. But all these programs cost money, and after opening their purse strings during the 8-year tenure of Pat Brown, Californians became more cautious about the state's direction. Race riots precipitated by police brutality in Los Angeles and student unrest over the Vietnam War in Berkeley and elsewhere also turned the voters against liberal Democrats such as Brown.

In 1966 Republican Ronald Reagan was elected governor. Reagan revived the California Republican party and moved the state in a more conservative direction before going on to serve as president. His successor as governor, Democrat Edmund G. "Jerry" Brown, Jr., was the son of the earlier Governor Brown and a liberal on social issues. Like Reagan, however, the younger Brown led California away from spending on growth-inducing infrastructure, such as highways and schools. In 1978 the voters solidified this change with the watershed tax-cutting initiative, Proposition 13 (see Chapter 8). Brown was followed by Republicans George Deukmejian in 1982 and Pete Wilson in 1990, each serving two terms in office. Wilson was initially seen as a moderate, but he moved to the right on welfare, illegal immigration, crime, and affirmative action to win re-election in 1994 and, in the process, alienated many minority voters from the Republican party. In 1998 California elected Gray Davis, its first Democratic governor in 16 years. He was re-elected in 2002 despite voter concerns about an energy crisis, a recession, and a growing budget deficit. As a consequence of these crises and his inability to resolve political gridlock on the budget, Davis faced an unprecedented recall election in October 2003. Voters chose to remove him from office and replace him with Republican Arnold Schwarzenegger.

California voters opted for Republicans in all but one presidential contest between 1948 and 1988 but have supported Democrats in every election since then. Democrats have had more consistent success in the state legislature and the congressional delegation, where they have been the dominant party since 1960. The voters have also been increasingly involved in policy making by initiative and referendum (see Chapter 2). Amendments to California's constitution, which require voter approval, appear on almost every state ballot. As a consequence, California's 1879 constitution has been amended nearly 500 times; the U.S. Constitution includes just 27 amendments.

Throughout these changes, the state continued to grow, outpacing most other states so much that the California delegation to the U.S. House of Representatives now numbers 53–more than 21 other states combined. Much of this growth was the result of a new wave of immigration facilitated by changes in national immigration laws during the 1960s and 1970s. The racially discriminatory quotas introduced by the Progressives in 1924 were eliminated, and immigration from Asia increased greatly, especially from Southeast Asia after the Vietnam War. A national amnesty for illegal residents also enabled many Mexicans to gain citizenship and bring their families from Mexico. In all, 85 percent of the 6 million newcomers and births in California in the 1980s were Asian, Latino, or black.[1] Growth slowed in the 1990s as two million more people left the state than came to it from other states, but California's population continued to increase as a result of births and immigration from abroad. In 1990, whites were 57 percent of the state's population; by 2000, they were 47 percent.

Constantly increasing diversity enlivened California's culture and provided a steady flow of new workers, but it also increased tensions.

Some affluent Californians retreated to gated communities; others fled the state. Racial conflict broke out between gangs and in schools and prisons. As in difficult economic times throughout California's history, a recession and recurring state budget deficits in the early 1990s led many Californians, including Governor Wilson, to blame immigrants, especially those who were in California illegally. A series of ballot measures raised divisive, race-related issues such as illegal immigration, bilingualism, and affirmative action. Some of the same issues arose during the recession that started in 2001 and during the recall election in 2003, but while tensions persisted, changing public attitudes, new leadership, and the increased electoral clout of minorities muted these issues to some extent.

CALIFORNIA TODAY

If California were an independent nation, its economy would rank sixth or seventh in the world, with an annual gross national product exceeding $1.4 trillion. Much of the state's strength stems from its economic diversity (Table 1.2). The elements of this diversity constitute powerful political interests in state politics.

Half of California–mostly desert and mountains–is owned by the state and federal governments, but a few big farm corporations control

TABLE 1.2
CALIFORNIA'S ECONOMY

INDUSTRIAL SECTOR	EMPLOYEES	AMOUNT (IN BILLIONS)
Agriculture, forestry, and fisheries	451,039	$24.435
Mining	23,842	8.623
Construction	797,563	57.712
Manufacturing	1,753,763	163.841
Transportation, utilities, and communications	940,601	92.421
Wholesale trade	650,521	89.384
Retail trade	1,565,701	127.073
Finance, insurance, and real estate	834,015	317.481
Services	5,584,467	326.119
Government (includes schools)	2,293,228	152.176
Total, all sectors	14,894,741	1,344.623

SOURCE: California Employment Development Department, June 2004, www.edd.ca.gov; and U.S. Department of Commerce, Bureau of Economic Analysis, Survey of Current Business, June 2004.

the state's rich farmlands. These enormous corporate farms, known as agribusinesses, make California the nation's leading farm state, producing more than 200 crops and providing 45 percent of the fruits and vegetables and 25 percent of the table food consumed nationally. Fresno County alone produces more farm products than 24 states combined.

State politics affects this huge economic force in many ways, but most notably in labor relations, environmental regulation, and water supply. Farmers and their employees have battled since the turn of the century over issues ranging from wages to safety. Under the leadership of Cesar Chavez and the United Farm Workers union, laborers organized and, supported by public boycotts of certain farm products, achieved some victories for workers, but the struggle continues today. California's agricultural industry is also caught up in environmental issues, including the use of harmful pesticides, the pollution of water supplies, and the urbanization of farmland as booming growth in the Central Valley absorbs farmland and brings urban problems such as traffic to rural areas. The biggest issue, however, is always water. Most of California's cities and farmlands must import water from other parts of the state. Thanks to government subsidies, farmers claim 80 percent of the state's water supply at prices so low that they have little reason to improve inefficient irrigation systems. Meanwhile, urban dwellers are asked to ration water during droughts, and the growth of urban areas is limited by their water supplies. Whether the issue is water, the environment, or labor relations, agriculture is in the thick of California politics as the state strives to protect an essential and powerful industry as well as the interests of its citizens.

Agriculture is big business, but many more Californians work in manufacturing, especially in the aerospace, defense, and high-tech industries. Even more people are employed in postindustrial occupations such as retail sales, finance, tourism, and services. Government policies on growth, the environment, and taxation affect all of these employment sectors, and all suffer when any one sector goes into a slump.

The defense industry did just that in the early 1990s, when the federal government reduced spending on expensive military programs and bases after the collapse of communism in the Soviet Union and the end of the Cold War. Suddenly, the state had to absorb 17 percent of the defense reductions. Retrenchment cost 175,000 defense-related jobs between 1988 and 1995, amounting to 55 percent of the entire industry sector.[2] Adjusted for inflation, military spending in California today is half what it was in 1988. This negative "peace dividend" coincided with a national recession that encouraged other manufacturers to flee California for states with lower taxes and wages. Altogether, more than 800,000 jobs were lost during the recession of the 1990s.[3]

Although some industries declined, others thrived, especially telecommunications, entertainment, medical equipment, international trade, and above all, high tech. Spawned by the defense and aerospace companies that fell into decline in the early 1990s, high tech was seen as the key to the economic revival of California and the nation at the end of the decade. These highly creative, research-oriented industries focus on computers, electronics, and information management and delivery systems.

At the peak of the high-tech boom, California hosted one fourth of the nation's high-tech firms, which provided nearly a million jobs. Half of the nation's computer engineers worked in what was dubbed **Silicon Valley,** named after the silicon chip that revolutionized the computer industry. Running between San Jose and San Francisco, Silicon Valley became a center for innovation in technology, from technical instruments, computer chips, networking equipment, workstations, and software to Internet-based "dot-com" businesses. Biomedical and pharmaceutical companies also boomed, further contributing to California's high-tech transformation. So productive was the area that in 1996 it surpassed New York as the top exporting region in the United States.

Computer technology also spurred rapid expansion of the entertainment industry, long a key component of California's economy. This particularly benefited the Los Angeles area, which had been hit hard by cuts in defense spending. Together, entertainment and tourism provide more than 500,000 jobs for Californians. Half of these are in film and television, but tourism remains a bastion of the economy, with California regularly ranking first among the states in visitors. Along with agriculture, high-tech, telecommunications, and other industries, these businesses made California a leader in both international and domestic trade. California's exports totaled $107 billion in 1999–more than 10 percent of the state's total business activity; 60 percent of this trade was technology related.[4]

However, the bubble burst in 2001 as the state and nation slumped into recession. Factors beyond California started the slide and the terrible events of September 11, 2001, exacerbated it, but California made its own unique contributions to what became a worldwide recession. First, the California-centered Internet boom went bust as thousands of dot-com companies failed to generate projected profits. The entire high-tech industry went into decline, and thousands of workers lost their jobs. At about the same time, an energy crisis hit California. The state had deregulated energy suppliers in 1996 at the urging of industry, but by 2000, prices for gas and electricity had risen and parts of the state experienced shortages of electrical power. The crisis climaxed in the summer of 2001, when Governor Gray Davis directed the state to purchase electricity supplies in advance and to accelerate the construction of more than 40 new power plants. These actions resolved the crisis for the moment, but Governor Davis's initial caution and the exorbitant prices the state paid for its advance purchases caused his popularity to slump. Like the Workingmen's party and the Progressives before them, some political leaders called for greater regulation or even public ownership of power supplies.

California was soon mired in recession, and unemployment reached 7 percent statewide and 9 percent in Silicon Valley (the national rate was 5.9 percent) in 2003. Silicon Valley alone lost 200,000 jobs–about 20 percent of its total job base. Economic historians pointed out that this was the most jobs lost by a metropolitan area since the Great Depression.[5] The impact of the recession was exacerbated when California industries moved jobs to other states or countries where they could operate more profitably. In 2002, Texas passed California as the nation's biggest exporter.

Soaring stock values during the tech boom had produced a surge in tax revenues for California. Governor Davis and the legislature busily expanded programs and cut some fees and taxes. But when the boom ended, tax revenues declined precipitously, producing a state budget deficit exceeding $20 billion. The deficit and other issues plunged California into a crisis that continued beyond the recall of Governor Davis in 2003. But California has suffered recessions before and recovered, thanks to the diversity of its economy and its people and their ability to adapt to change. Most other states lack these advantages; some are dependent on a single industry or product, and none can match the energy and optimism brought by California's constant flow of immigrants. By 2004, California's economy seemed to be bouncing back, even in Silicon Valley.

California's adaptability may derive from a population even more varied than its economy. The constant flow of immigrants brings workers eager to take jobs in the state's new and old industries. California attracted nearly 25 percent of all immigrants to the United States in 2000, and as of that year, 26 percent of California's population was foreign born. Three fourths of recent immigrants are from Mexico or Asia; nearly 40 percent of all Californians over the age of 5 speak a language other than English at home. The extent of California's ethnic diversity, both now and in the future, is indicated in Table 1.3. Although non-Latino whites remain the single largest group, they are no longer a majority. Asian and Latino numbers have grown rapidly since the 1970s, while the black and white proportions of California's population have fallen. This shift is slowly producing a shift in political power as well.

TABLE 1.3

California's Racial and Ethnic Diversity: Past, Present, and Projected

	1990	2000	2010
Non-Latino white	57.1%	46.7%	44.8%
Latino	26.0	32.4	34.9
Asian/Pacific Islander	9.2	11.2	13.3
Black	7.1	6.4	6.4
Native American	0.6	0.5	0.6

SOURCE: U.S. Census. Percentage totals may exceed 100 due to rounding; 2000 totals do not include 2.7 percent of mixed race.

The realization of the California dream is not shared equally among these groups. In 2002 the income of 12.8 percent of Californians fell below the federal poverty level (compared with 12.1 percent nationwide). The gap between rich and poor in California is among the largest in the United States and is still growing. Poverty is worst among Latinos, blacks, and Southeast Asians, who tend to occupy the bottom of the class structure with low-paying service jobs; other Asians, along with Anglos, predominate in the more comfortable professional classes. The economic disparities are profound. Whereas the median household income in 2001 was $66,000 for whites and $62,000 for Asians, the median was $37,500 for Latinos and $50,000 for blacks. The 2000 census also reported that the gap between rich and poor grew in the 1990s.

The biggest economic problem for minorities, recent arrivals, and many other Californians today is the cost of housing. With a median price of $469,170 in 2004, California houses cost more than double the national average; only 19 percent of the state's families could afford to purchase the median-priced house, compared with a national average of 66 percent.[6] As a result, home ownership in California lags well behind the national average, and more Californians are driven into the rental market—where prices also exceed the national average. Health care is also a problem for poor and working Californians. Nineteen percent have no health insurance, although coverage expanded under the state's Healthy Families program, established in 2001.

Geographic divisions complicate California's economic and ethnic diversity. The most pronounced of these lies between north and south. The San Francisco Bay Area tends to be liberal and Democratic, with high concentrations of European and Asian ethnic groups. "The City" of San Francisco is a major financial center, whereas its more populous neighbor, San Jose, hosts the high-tech industries of Silicon Valley. Southern California originally drew mainly Midwestern immigrants, but today ethnic minorities outnumber Anglos in both the city and the county of Los Angeles. Although Los Angeles tends to vote Democratic, most of the rest of Southern California is staunchly Republican.

Rapid growth in other parts of California now challenges the predominance of the two great metropolitan areas. The state's vast Central Valley has led the way, with cities from Sacramento to Fresno and Bakersfield gobbling up farmland. The Inland Empire, from Riverside to San Bernardino, has grown even more rapidly in the last decade. Although still sparsely populated, California's northern coast, Sierra Nevada, and southern desert regions are also growing, while retaining their own distinct identities. Water, agriculture, and the environment are major issues in all these areas. Except for Sacramento, the Central Valley and these other regions of California are more conservative than their metropolitan counterparts. Their impact on state politics increased greatly in the 1990s.

INTO THE FUTURE

All these factors add up to California politics today. No wonder it seems complicated! From a history full of conflicting interests and turbulent change, California has forged unique political institutions, including the ability of the electorate to make policy and recall officeholders via direct democracy. All the elements of today's economic, demographic, and geographic diversity vie with one another for political influence within the framework they have inherited, sometimes trying to change it. Just as the economic and demographic changes of the past have shaped contemporary California, so today's changes are shaping the future.

Notes

1. U.S. Census.
2. "The 'Silver' Age of State's Defense-Aerospace Economy," *Los Angeles Times,* July 7, 1996, pp. M1, M6.
3. *New York Times,* March 29, 1995.
4. California Trade and Commerce Agency.
5. "Survey of California," *The Economist,* May 1, 2004, p. 9.
6. California Association of Realtors.

Learn More on the World Wide Web

The California Constitution Online:

www.leginfo.ca.gov/const-toc.html

Demographic data:

California Department of Finance: www.dof.ca.gov

RAND: www.ca.rand.org

U.S. Census: www.census.gov

Learn More at the Library

Carey McWilliams, *California: The Great Exception,* Berkeley: University of California Press, 1949 (or any of his other books).

Frank Norris, *The Octopus,* New York: Penguin, 1901. A novel of nineteenth-century California.

Kevin Starr, *California Dream Series,* Oxford: Oxford University Press. A series of books covering California history from 1850 to date.

Chapter 2

POLITICAL PARTIES AND DIRECT DEMOCRACY: TOO MUCH DEMOCRACY?

In most states, political parties link citizens and government. Their most important tasks are to build coalitions of different interests and help candidates make their case to the voters. This doesn't always happen in California, where party organizations are weak and the electorate itself can make policy. As noted in Chapter 1, the Progressive reformers attempted to rid California of the railroad-dominated political machines and bosses of the nineteenth century by weakening political parties. In the resulting power vacuum, personal appeal, skillful media manipulation, and well-financed campaigns have become as important as the political party labels attached to individual candidates, and sometimes more so.

The Progressives also introduced direct democracy. Through the initiative, referendum, and recall, the voters were given the power to make law and even to overrule leaders or to remove them between elections. Contrary to the reformers' intent, however, interest groups and politicians have learned to use–and sometimes abuse–the process.

Weak political parties and direct democracy are fixtures of the state constitution and remain very much a part of modern California politics. Some political observers argue that the result promotes political disarray, governmental gridlock, and voters who are confused or turned off. Others believe that the system reflects a political value system that eschews organization and structured authority and maximizes opportunities for democratic decision making.

THE PROGRESSIVE LEGACY

To challenge the dominance of the Southern Pacific Railroad's political machine, Progressive reformers from both the Democratic and Republican parties focused on the machine's control of party conventions, where candidates were nominated for office. Republican reformers scored the first breakthrough in 1908 by getting many anti-railroad candidates nominated and elected to the state legislature. In 1909 the reform legislators replaced party conventions with **primary elections,** in which the registered voters of each party choose the nominee. Candidates who win their party's primary in these elections face the nominees of other parties in the November **general election.** By instituting this system, the reformers ended the Southern Pacific railroad's monopoly in the nomination process.

In 1910 the Progressives elected a reform governor and legislature. They introduced **direct democracy**–the initiative, referendum, and recall–to give policy-making authority to the people. They replaced the party column ballot–which had permitted block voting for all the candidates of a single party by making just one mark–with separate balloting for each office. They also introduced **cross-filing,** a voting method that permitted candidates of one party to seek the nominations of rival parties. Finally, the Progressives made the election of judges, school board members, and local government officials **nonpartisan** by eliminating party labels for these contests.

These changes reduced the railroad's control of the political parties, but they also sapped the strength of the party organizations. By allowing the voters to circumvent an unresponsive legislature, direct democracy paved the way for interest groups to dominate policy making. Deletion of the party column ballot encouraged voters to cast their ballots for members of different parties for different offices (split-ticket voting), increasing the likelihood of a divided-party government (see Chapter 7). Nonpartisan local elections made it difficult for the parties to build their organizations at the grassroots level.

Parties tried to regain control of nominations by settling on favored candidates before the primary elections. This effort developed largely through unofficial party organizations, such as the California Republican Assembly (formed in 1935) and the California Democratic Council (formed in 1953), whose influences peaked during the 1960s, prompting the legislature to outlaw such **preprimary endorsements.** Meanwhile, in 1959, the legislature, controlled by Democratic majorities for the first time in more than 40 years, outlawed cross-filing, which had been disproportionately helpful to Republican incumbents, and returned to the system where only party members could select their nominee.

California traditionally held primary elections in June, close to the times of the primaries of the other states. However, during the 1980s many states moved their primaries to earlier in the year, giving them more say over presidential nominations. To counter that influence, California moved its presidential primary to March for the 1996 election, but gained little because eight other states shifted their primaries to even earlier dates. When the state's March presidential primaries in 2000 and

2004 had no significant impact, the legislature moved California's primary elections back to June beginning in 2006.

PARTY ORGANIZATION–STRUCTURE AND SUPPORTERS

As a result of the Progressive changes, political parties in California operate under unusual constraints. Although the original reformers have long since departed from the scene, the reform mentality remains very much a part of California's political culture.

THE OFFICIAL PARTY STRUCTURE

According to the California State Elections Code, political parties can place candidates on the ballot by registering a number of members equal to 1 percent of the state vote in the most recent gubernatorial election or by submitting a petition with signatures amounting to 10 percent of that vote. After a party is qualified, if it retains the registration of at least 1 percent of the voters or if at least one of its candidates for any statewide office receives 2 percent of the votes cast, that party will be on the ballot in the next election. By virtue of their sizes, the Democratic and Republican parties have been fixtures on the ballot almost since statehood.

Minor parties, sometimes called **third parties,** are another story. Some have been on the ballot for decades; others have had brief political lives. In 1996, for example, the Reform and Natural Law parties attained ballot status by petition. Although qualifying for the ballot is relatively easy for new parties, breaking the hold of the two major political parties has proved difficult. In the 2002 general election, the Green, American Independent, Natural Law, and Libertarian parties each secured the minimum 2 percent of the vote for one of their statewide candidates, guaranteeing them positions on the ballot in 2004. The Reform party failed to capture the minimum and lost its ballot status. So did the Peace and Freedom party, which began as an anti–Vietnam War party in 1968, but it requalified in 2003 by registering enough new voters to exceed the minimum required by state law. Seven parties thus appeared on California's 2004 ballot. Among these parties, the Greens have been the most successful at winning elections, including one state legislator and several local officials.

Despite the presence of several parties on the ballot, the two major parties dominate the state's political landscape. The Democratic and Republican presidential candidates garnered 99 percent of the vote in 2004, slightly less than the 96 percent shared by the Democratic and Republican candidates for governor in 2002.

California voters choose their party when they register to vote, which must be done 15 days or more before the election. In 2004, 79 percent were signed up as either Democrats or Republicans. Five percent signed up with the other parties, and 16 percent declared themselves independent (officially known as "decline to state"). The independent percentage has been rising since 1986, when it stood at 9 percent.

California has traditionally had a **closed primary** system. Voters who are registered with a political party can cast their ballots in the primary only for that party's nominees for various offices. All are free to cast ballots for any party's candidates in the November general election. This system changed briefly in 1996, when a voter-approved initiative introduced the **open primary,** which allowed voters to support any listed candidate for each office irrespective of the voters' party affiliations. Proponents praised this new method as an opportunity for voters to nominate the best-qualified individuals; opponents countered that the system would allow voters of one party to pick the candidates of the other–possibly "setting up" a weak nominee who could easily be defeated. But the U.S. Supreme Court declared that the open primary, as defined by the initiative, violated the First Amendment rights of the state's political parties. California returned to its closed primary system in 2002 with a slight modification. Previously, voters not registered with a political party could vote only on propositions and nonpartisan offices. In 2002 and 2004, they were also allowed to choose to vote in the primary election of one of the parties. Then in November 2004 the voters faced two competing measures–one keeping the closed primary, another reinstating the open primary. This time they stayed with the closed primary and rejected the open primary proposal.

Before the Great Depression, California was steadfastly Republican, but during the 1930s voters here, like those in many other states, forged a Democratic majority. Since then the Democrats have dominated in voter registration (Figure 2.1), although their lead has declined from a peak of 60 percent in 1942 to 43.2 percent in 2004. Republicans have gained from this slippage, but the "decline to state" category has grown the most. Registration patterns and voting practices often differ markedly, however. For example, despite their registration margin, the Democrats did not gain a majority in both houses of the state legislature until 1958. More dramatically, Republican candidates have won 6 of the last 10 gubernatorial elections.

As with registration and voting, state law dictates party organization. Today's Democratic and Republican parties have similar structures, although the Democrats elect a few more party officials. The state **central committee,** with about 1,000 members, is the highest-ranking body in each party. All party candidates and officeholders are automatically members, along with county chairpersons. The Democrats also elect members from each assembly district. Each party's state central committee elects

FIGURE 2.1

PARTY REGISTRATION DURING GUBERNATORIAL ELECTION YEARS

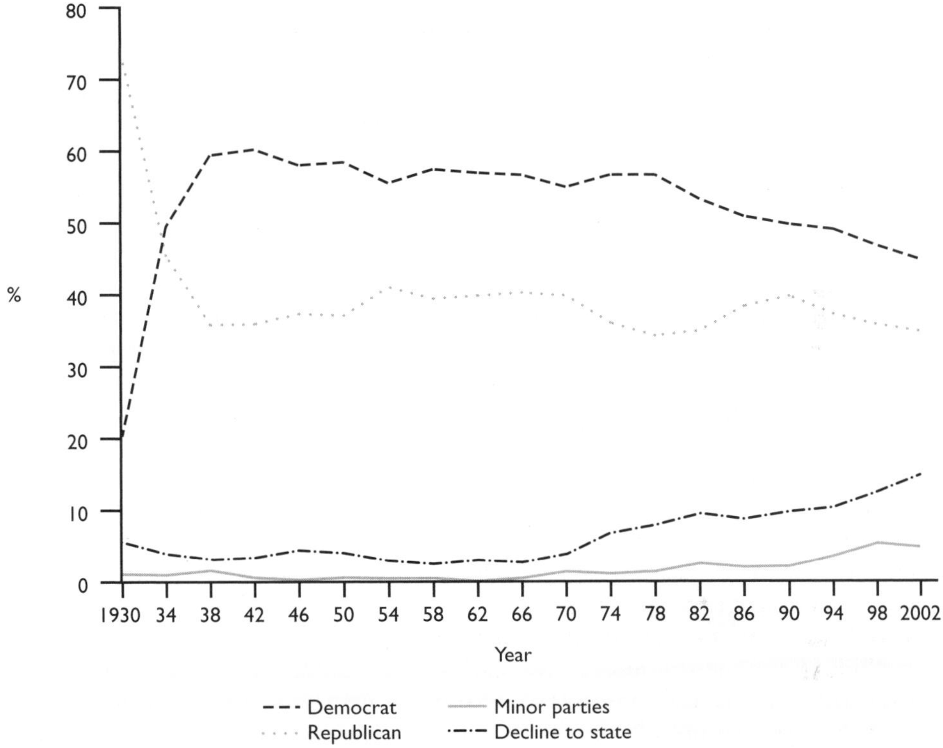

SOURCE: California Secretary of State.

a state chair, but the position must alternate between Northern and Southern California every 2 years. Although the position traditionally has been powerless, competition for it is often intense.

Beneath the state central committees are county central committees. The voters registered with each party choose committee members every 2 years in the primary election. Officeholders are also members, which, critics say, enables incumbents to dominate the grassroots members, but the overlapping membership of officeholders, nominees, and county chairs is the only link between the county and state levels of the party. The Progressive reforms rendered California's political parties next to impotent, denying meaningful roles to official organizations and their central committees in preprimary endorsements or fundraising. Nevertheless, county central committees sometimes engage in intense conflict among activists. Liberals usually dominate Democratic county central committees, whereas conservatives enjoy disproportionate power in Republican committees. The religious right gained influence in the Republican party in the 1990s by organizing to take over a majority of the party's county central committees. Recently, moderate Republicans have successfully challenged their control in some counties.

California's political parties got a chance to strengthen their role in choosing party nominees (a major source of their weakness) when the U.S. Supreme Court overturned the state ban on preprimary endorsements of candidates by political parties in 1990. California Democrats responded quickly by establishing a preprimary endorsement process that required a candidate to secure at least 60 percent of the delegates at their state convention, but the Republican party has officially declined to utilize preprimary endorsements.

Despite assertions of better party organization, preprimary endorsements have mattered little to California voters. Of 16 statewide candidates officially endorsed by the Democrats in primaries since the court ruling, nine were incumbents certain of victory and four of the others failed to win their party's nomination. Whether the preprimary endorsement will strengthen the parties is doubtful because California's weak parties are a consequence not only of state law but also of fickle voter loyalty to the parties, high-spending campaigns, and the media.

PARTY SUPPORTERS

Activists in the official and unofficial party organizations make up less than 5 percent of the electorate. The remaining support base comes from citizens who designate their party affiliations when they register to vote and usually cast their ballots accordingly. Public opinion polls tell us that voters who prefer the Democratic party tend to be sympathetic to the poor and immigrants, concerned about the environment, in favor of gay rights, gun control, and abortion rights, and supportive of tax increases to provide public services. Those who prefer the Republican party are more likely to oppose these views and to worry more about big government and high taxes. Of course, many people mix these positions.[1]

Both major parties enjoy widespread support, but the more liberal Democratic party fares better with blacks, city dwellers, union members, and residents of Los Angeles, Sacramento, and the San Francisco Bay Area. Central California was once dominated by the Democrats, but increasingly the region has become a battleground for the two major parties. Latino voters have also traditionally favored Democrats, a tendency that has been strengthened by Republican support for several statewide initiatives on welfare, immigration, affirmative action, and bilingual education. Most Asian nationalities identify themselves as Democratic, but some (notably Chinese and Vietnamese) lean Republican. Chinese, Vietnamese, and Asian Indians are also more likely to register as independents than are other Californians. As with Latinos, Asian loyalties to the California Republican party were weakened by its sponsorship of initiatives perceived as anti-immigrant in the 1990s. Thanks in large part to the failure of Republicans to win support from minority voters, Democrats currently enjoy majorities in the state legislature and congressional delegation and control of all statewide offices except one.

The more conservative Republican party does better with whites, suburbanites, residents of rural areas, and Southern Californians (except in Los Angeles), as well as with older, more affluent voters and with Christian conservatives. Together these constituencies are the most dependable voters, which is one reason why Republicans have won elections in California despite their registration disadvantage. Republican strategist Stuart Spencer, however, warns, "The general electorate has gone exactly the other way from the party leadership in terms of positions on immigration, ethnicity, abortion, guns. Till they get their ship righted, and move back to a more centrist, moderate position, they're going to have trouble."[2]

In the past, Republican candidates were also successful because they could often win the support of Democratic voters. Cross-filing (until 1958), charismatic candidates, clever campaigns, and weak party organizations made "split-ticket" voting common in California, with Democrats sometimes supporting Republican candidates and vice versa. But in the 1990s, ticket splitting declined, and instead, voters increasingly voted a straight party-line ticket–either all Democratic or all Republican.[3] With more voters registered Democratic than Republican, Democrats seemed assured of victories indefinitely. But this assumption was challenged when many Democrats voted for Arnold Schwarzenegger for governor in the 2003 recall election. Schwarzenegger proved that a moderate Republican could win the votes of both Democrats and independents. His party had simply not offered such a candidate in the 1990s. It remains to be seen whether it will do so in the future.

DIRECT DEMOCRACY

Party politics is not the only way in which Californians participate in the political process. To counter the railroad machine's control of state and local government, the Progressive reformers also guaranteed the people some say through the mechanisms of direct democracy introduced in Chapter 1: the recall, the referendum, and the initiative.

Each statewide initiative or referendum is assigned a number by the secretary of state; local issues are assigned letters by the county clerk. Propositions once started with the number 1 in each election, but beginning in 1983, to prevent confusion, they continued in sequence up to Proposition 227 in June 1998. In November of that year, numbering started over again with Proposition 1.

THE RECALL

The least-used form of direct democracy is the **recall,** a means by which the voters can remove officeholders at all levels of government between scheduled elections. Recall advocates circulate a petition with a statement of their reasons, which can be anything at all. They must collect a specific number of voter signatures within a specific time period (the numbers vary with the office in question). At the local level, for example, the number of signatures required to qualify a recall for the ballot varies between 10 and 30 percent of those who voted in the previous local election; these must be collected over periods that vary between 40 and 160 days. A recall petition for a judge or a legislator requires signatures equaling 20 percent of the vote in the last state election, while for state executive officeholders the number is 12 percent. In all these cases, petitioners have 160 days to collect the signatures. If enough signatures are collected by advocates and validated by the secretary of state (for a state officeholder) or by the county clerk (for a local officeholder), an election is held. The ballot is simple: "Shall [name] be removed from the office of [title]?" The recall takes effect if a majority of voters vote yes, and then either an election or an appointment, whichever state or local law requires, fills the vacancy for the office. Elected officials who are recalled cannot be candidates in the replacement election.

Recalling state officeholders is easier in California than in the other 17 states where recall is possible. All but one of these states require more signatures, and while any reason suffices in California, most other states require corruption or malfeasance by the officeholder. Nevertheless, recalls are rare in California, where the recall has been used most extensively and successfully in local government, particularly by parents who are angry with school boards. Even so, only a dozen or so recalls are on local ballots in any given year and only about half of the officials who face recall are removed from office. Two state senators were recalled in 1913, but no other state officeholders were removed until 1995, when two legislators were recalled during a struggle between Democrats and Republicans over control of the state assembly.

Then, spectacularly, Governor Gray Davis was recalled in 2003. Davis had narrowly won re-election in November 2002, but three months later opponents launched their recall petition. Thirty-one previous attempts to recall a California governor had failed to make the ballot, however, and most political observers assumed that the petitioners would fail to acquire the 897,158 valid signatures required to qualify for an election. But they underestimated voter discontent, not only with Davis but also with the general state of California politics. Despite his re-election, Davis's approval rating in public opinion polls had sunk to just 24 percent when signature gathering began.[4] His decline in popularity was the result of a combination of factors that included his lackadaisical leadership during the state's energy crisis in 2001, the recession, the resultant huge budget deficit, and the apparent inability of the legislature and the governor to agree on a solution to these problems. Davis's reserved personality, distinctly lacking in charisma, also contributed to his problems. When his opponents launched their recall, they discovered a groundswell of support, facilitated by conservative talk radio hosts and the availability of the Internet to circulate petitions. Even so, signature gathering was slow until Republican Congressman Darrell Issa contributed $2 million to pay for professionals to assist.

On July 23, Secretary of State Kevin Shelley certified that 1.3 million valid signatures had been gathered, far more than the 897,158 required. On July 25, Lieutenant Governor Cruz Bustamante set an election for October 7. Within days, hundreds of people filed to run as replacement candidates. One hundred and thirty-five qualified to run, including actor Arnold Schwarzenegger. The 75-day campaign took the state by storm, gaining far more media and public attention than any regular election in recent memory–thanks in part to the presence of a movie-star candidate. On October 7, 55.4 percent of the voters said "yes" to recall and Schwarzenegger easily outpaced all other replacement candidates with 48.6 percent of the vote. For the first time in California history–and only the second time in U.S. history–a governor had been recalled.

Has California set a new trend? Will other officeholders in California and elsewhere soon face recalls? It's possible, but it seems more likely that the unique set of circumstances that brought about the fall of Gray Davis–the energy crisis, the recession, the budget deficit, legislative gridlock, and Davis's own unpopularity–will not be readily replicated. Nevertheless, the voters had flexed their muscles, and other officeholders had been put on notice.

THE REFERENDUM

The **referendum** is another form of direct democracy. A referendum allows the electors to nullify statutes enacted by the legislature. Advocates of a referendum have 90 days to collect a number of signatures equal to 5 percent of the votes cast for governor in the previous election (373,816, based on the 2002 vote). Referenda are even more rare than recalls. Only 39 of 52 attempts to qualify referenda for the ballot have succeeded; voters approved 25 of these. In 2004, business groups qualified a referendum on health-care legislation approved in Governor Davis's last days in office. The hard-fought campaign pitted liberals, unions, and Democrats who supported the program against conservatives, business leaders, and

Republicans, including Governor Arnold Schwarzenegger. In the end, the voters narrowly rejected the health-care legislation, even though nearly 20 percent of Californians lack health insurance.

THE INITIATIVE

Recalls and referenda are reactions to what elected officials do; in contrast, the **initiative** allows voters to make policy themselves. They can do so by drafting a new law or a constitutional amendment and then circulating petitions to get it onto the ballot. Qualifying a proposed law requires a number of signatures equal to 5 percent of the votes cast for governor in the last election; constitutional amendments require a number of signatures equal to 8 percent (598,105, based on the 2002 election). If enough valid signatures are obtained within 150 days, the initiative goes to the voters at the next election or, on rare occasions, in a special election called by the governor.

Initiatives tend to be the most controversial measures on the ballot. Their subjects vary wildly. In the last few years, Californians have voted on property-tax limits, minimum-wage hikes, capital punishment, affirmative action, gun control, AIDS quarantines, insurance reforms, illegal immigration, and Indian casinos, to name a few. Voters have twice rejected initiative proposals for school vouchers that would have set aside public funds to be spent on children in schools (public or private) designated by their parents. In 1998, voters passed limits on bilingual education and banned the slaughter of horses for human consumption. In 2000, the electorate voted to define marriage as a relationship between a man and a woman only. And in 2004, voters made decisions about issues ranging from tribal gambling (again) to stem-cell research, DNA sampling, and mental-health services.

Twenty-four other states provide for the initiative, but few rely on it as heavily as California. The use of initiatives flourished between 1912 and 1939, but was less common during the next 4 decades. Then political consultants and special interest groups rediscovered the initiative, and ballot measures proliferated. The 1988 and 1990 election year ballots witnessed an explosion, with 18 initiatives on each. In 2002, the March and November elections combined presented only five initiatives, but 11 were on the November 2004 ballot (Table 2.1).

LEGISLATIVE "INITIATIVES," CONSTITUTIONAL AMENDMENTS, AND BONDS

Propositions can also be placed on the ballot by the state legislature. These often equal or exceed the number of citizen-generated initiatives. Such **legislative initiatives** can include new laws that the legislature prefers to put before the voters rather than enact on its own or proposed constitutional amendments for which voter approval is compulsory. Voter

TABLE 2.1
THE TRACK RECORD OF STATE INITIATIVES

TIME PERIOD	NUMBER	NUMBER ADOPTED	NUMBER REJECTED
1912–1919	31	8	23
1920–1929	34	10	24
1930–1939	37	10	27
1940–1949	20	7	13
1950–1959	11	1	10
1960–1969	10	3	7
1970–1979	24	7	17
1980–1989	52	25	27
1990–1999	50	20	30
2000–2004	33	12	21
Totals	302	103 (34%)	199 (66%)

SOURCE: California Secretary of State.

approval is also required when the governor or the legislature wishes to borrow money to finance parks, schools, transportation, or other capital-intensive projects through the sale of bonds (state IOUs). Few of these proposals are controversial, and more than 60 percent are passed. In 2002, for example, voters approved five bonds totaling $21.8 billion for new schools, parks, water projects, and housing. In 2004, Governor Arnold Schwarzenegger persuaded the legislature to put a $15-billion bond before the voters to help balance the budget. Schwarzenegger and Democratic leaders campaigned hard for the measure and ultimately won voter approval.

Most legislative initiatives are on the ballot because the legislature cannot amend the constitution or borrow money without public approval. Sometimes, however, the legislature turns to the voters because lawmakers don't want to make controversial policy without public support. This was the case in 1993, when voters were asked to make permanent a then-temporary half-cent addition to the state sales tax.

THE POLITICS OF BALLOT PROPOSITIONS

The recent proliferation of ballot propositions is hardly the result of a sudden surge in democratic participation. Rather, it stems largely from the opportunism of special interests, individual politicians, and public relations firms. California's state lottery, for example, was virtually the creation of a single company that paid for the circulation of petitions and then funded the campaign that sold the proposition to the voters. Perhaps the most common topic of ballot measures generated by specific interest groups in recent years has been the regulation of gambling on tribal lands, as gaming interests attempt to maximize profits and competing interests seek to limit such gambling or to obtain a share of the profits for the state. Two such measures were on the November 2004 ballot.

State ballot propositions can be costly endeavors. Although intended as mechanisms for grassroots citizen groups to shape policy, even the most grassroots-driven initiatives cost half a million dollars to qualify, and millions more are required to mount a successful campaign. The harsh truth is that it takes money to reach California's millions of voters. Even with the massive public disillusionment with Governor Gray Davis, the recall might never have qualified for the ballot if Republican Congressman Darrell Issa had not provided $2 million to pay for signature gathering.

Once a measure qualifies for the ballot, even more money is spent. Campaigns for and against the 14 propositions on the ballot in 1998 cost $227.1 million, up 61 percent from the $141.3 million spent in 1996. Campaigns for and against just one ballot measure on tribal gambling paid out $96 million–the most ever spent on a single proposition in California history. Sometimes initiatives are funded primarily by wealthy individuals, such as international financier George Soros (drug decriminalization) and high-tech executive Tim Draper (school vouchers). Politicians have also discovered initiatives as a way to further their own careers or shape public policy. For example, Republican Governor Pete Wilson helped secure re-election in 1994 by sponsoring a successful measure on illegal immigration. In 2002, movie star Arnold Schwarzenegger sponsored an initiative to fund afterschool programs, advancing both that cause and his own political career.

Public relations firms and political consultants–virtual "guns for hire"–have developed lucrative careers from managing initiative and referenda campaigns. One consultant, for example, made more than $2 million working for the "Yes on 5" Indian casino initiative in 1998 simply for obtaining enough signatures to qualify the proposal for the ballot.[5] Other specialists offer expertise in public-opinion polling, computer-targeted mailing, and television advertising–the staples of modern campaigns. Some firms generate initiatives themselves by conducting test mailings and preliminary polls in hopes of snagging big contracts from proposition sponsors. With millions of dollars in campaign spending hanging in the balance, big economic interests gain an advantage over grassroots efforts–surely not what the Progressives intended.

Nevertheless, direct democracy offers hope to the relatively powerless by enabling them to take their case to the public over the opposition of elected officials. In 1998, entertainer Rob Reiner led a successful effort to add 50 cents to the price of each pack of cigarettes, with the additional money directed to children's health programs. Tobacco allies spent more than $30 million against Proposition 10, compared with less than $10 million spent by the advocates. That such groups can beat long odds and the state's political establishment only increases the attractiveness of initiatives.

Unfortunately, direct democracy does not necessarily result in good laws. Because self-interested sponsors draft initiatives and media masters run campaigns, careful and rational deliberation is rare. Flaws or contradictions in successful initiatives may take years to resolve. Sometimes this is done through the implementation of the measures by government agencies or through the legislative process. Increasingly, however, disputes about initiatives are tested in state and federal courts, which must rule on whether they are consistent with other laws and with the state and federal constitutions. In recent years, courts have overturned all or parts of initiatives dealing with illegal immigration and campaign finance, for example. Although such rulings seem to deny the will of the voters, the courts are doing their jobs. Even the voters cannot make laws that contradict the state or federal constitutions.

The increased use of direct democracy has also had an impact on the power of our elected representatives. Although we expect them to make policy, their ability to do so has been constrained by a sequence of initiatives in recent decades. This is particularly the case with the state budget, much of which is dictated by past ballot measures rather than the legislature or the governor.

The proliferation of initiatives, expensive and deceptive campaigns, flawed laws, and court interventions have annoyed voters and policy makers alike. Perhaps as a consequence, two thirds of all initiatives are rejected (Table 2.1). Nevertheless, a solid majority of respondents to statewide surveys "believe that policy decisions made through the initiative process are probably better than policy decisions made by the governor and legislature" and 76 percent view recall as a good thing. At the same time, substantial majorities favor reform of both mechanisms of direct democracy, requiring a higher percentage of signatures to qualify a recall and a review of ballot language and legal issues before initiatives are placed on the ballot.[6]

POLITICAL PARTIES, DIRECT DEMOCRACY, AND CALIFORNIA POLITICS

Direct democracy and weak political parties are basic to California politics. The direct primary maximizes voter choice among candidates; weak parties foster high-spending, candidate-centered campaigns that often seem to confuse or obscure voter choice. Candidates must rely on financial contributors to pay for campaigns that are not funded by the parties, thus enhancing the influence of individuals and groups with money. Direct democracy gives these same interests yet another way to advance their causes, and the proliferation of propositions further confounds voters. Does California have too much democracy? Sometimes it seems so. Some voters feel overwhelmed and turned off, but most manage to sift through complex initiatives and seductive campaigns to find the policies and candidates who suit their preferences.

Notes

1. Public Policy Institute of California, Statewide Survey, February 2004 (www.ppic.org).
2. *New York Times,* February 28, 2000.
3. See Gary C. Jacobson, "Partisanship in California Elections," paper for the Annual Meeting of the Western Political Science Association, 2002.
4. Public Policy Institute of California, "State of the Golden State," August 2003 (www.ppic.org).
5. *Sacramento Bee,* January 24, 1999, p. 1A.
6. "Just the Facts: Californians and the Initiative Process," Public Policy Institute of California, February 2001; Mark Baldassare, "Californians and Their Government," Public Policy Institute of California, January 2001; Public Policy Institute of California, Statewide Survey, October 2003 (all at www.ppic.org).

Learn More on the World Wide Web

About electoral systems:

Ballot Access News: http://www.ballot-access.org

About political parties:

American Independent Party: www.aipca.org

Democratic party: www.ca-dem.org

Green party: www.cagreens.org

Libertarian party: www.ca.lp.org

Natural Law party: www.natural-law.org

Peace and Freedom party: www.peaceandfreedom.org

Republican party: www.cagop.org

About ballot propositions:

www.calvoter.org

www.ss.ca.gov

Learn More at the Library

John Allswang, *The Initiative and Referendum in California, 1897–1998,* Stanford, CA: Stanford University Press, 2000.

Ann O'M. Bowman and Richard C. Kearney, *State and Local Government: The Essentials,* New York: Houghton Mifflin Company, 2000.

Elisabeth R. Gerber et al., *Stealing the Initiative,* Upper Saddle River, NJ: Prentice Hall, 2001.

Larry N. Gerston and Terry Christensen, *Recall! California's Political Earthquake,* Armonk, NY: M. E. Sharpe, 2004.

Jim Shultz, *The Initiative Cookbook,* San Francisco: The Democracy Center, 1996.

CHAPTER 3

VOTERS, CANDIDATES, CAMPAIGNS, AND THE MEDIA: THE MIX OF MONEY AND MARKETING

A typical California ballot requires voters to make decisions about more than 20 elective positions and propositions. Even the best-informed citizens sometimes find it difficult to choose among candidates for offices they know little about and to decide on obscure and complicated propositions. Because political parties provide little guidance, candidates, campaigns, and the media play crucial roles in this process in California.

Campaigns and the media are also important because of the mobility and rootlessness that characterize California society. More than half of all Californians were born elsewhere, and as many as one third of the voters in every state election are participating for the first time. Residents also move frequently within the state, reducing the political influence of families, friends, and peer groups and boosting that of campaigns and the media.

THE VOTERS

California residents who are 18 years or older are eligible to vote unless they are in prison or a mental institution. New voters must register at least 15 days before an election by completing a simple form available at public places such as post offices, fire stations, and shopping centers, where party activists eagerly solicit new voters. Registration forms are also provided with applications for driver's licenses and at social service agencies. Today, new voters can even register online.

Altogether, nearly 22 million Californians are eligible to vote, but only 15 million register and fewer than 10 million actually vote. That's less than half of all those eligible–close to the national average. In the gubernatorial election of 2002, turnout among those registered to vote was 58 percent, while turnout reached 61 percent in the hard-fought recall election of 2003. Turnout is usually higher in presidential elections, and in 2004, just over 68 percent of the state's registered voters participated, a rate that was nevertheless lower than the national average. Although most voters cast their ballots at designated polling places, over 25 percent of the California electorate votes by mail, having requested **absentee ballots** from their county registrar of voters. Some vote "absentee" because they expect to be away from home or will be too busy on election day, others do so because they want to deal with the complex ballots at their leisure, and still others vote absentee because campaigns push identified supporters to vote by mail to ensure their participation. Voters who prefer to cast their ballots this way can sign up as "permanent" absentee voters so they don't have to request an absentee ballot for every election.

Why do so many Californians neglect to vote? Some people don't get around to registering. Some are too busy on election day. Some are apathetic, some are unaware, and others feel too uninformed to act. Still others believe that voting is a charade because "it's all rigged" or "the candidates are all alike." Some people are bewildered by all the messages that bombard them during a typical California election. But the reason that people most frequently give for not voting is that they are too busy.

Yet political campaigns are designed to motivate voters to support candidates and causes. This task is complicated because those who vote are not a representative cross section of the actual population. Non-Latino whites, for example, make up 46.7 percent of the population but over 70 percent of the electorate. Although Latinos, African Americans, and Asians constitute 53.3 percent of California's population, they are less than 30 percent of the voters in primary and general elections.[1] This disparity in turnout means that California's voting electorate is not representative of the state's population. The lower participation rate among Latinos and Asians is mostly explained by the relative youth of these populations (about one third of Latinos, for example, are too young to vote) and by the fact that many are not yet citizens. Language, culture, and socioeconomic status may also be barriers to registration and voting among minority groups. Over time this will change, however. Latino turnout, for example, has more than trebled since 1990, rising from 4 percent of the electorate to 14 percent in 2000,[2] due largely to Republican attacks on immigrants and affirmative action that resulted in a surge of Democratic voters.

Differences in the levels of participation do not end with ethnicity. The people most likely to vote are suburbanites and Republicans who are richer, better educated, and older. Lower levels of participation are usually found among poorer, less educated, and younger inner-city residents and Democrats. According to recent reports, 93 percent of people over the age of 65 are registered to vote and nearly 70 percent vote, while

FIGURE 3.1

POLITICAL PARTICIPATION BY ETHNIC GROUPS

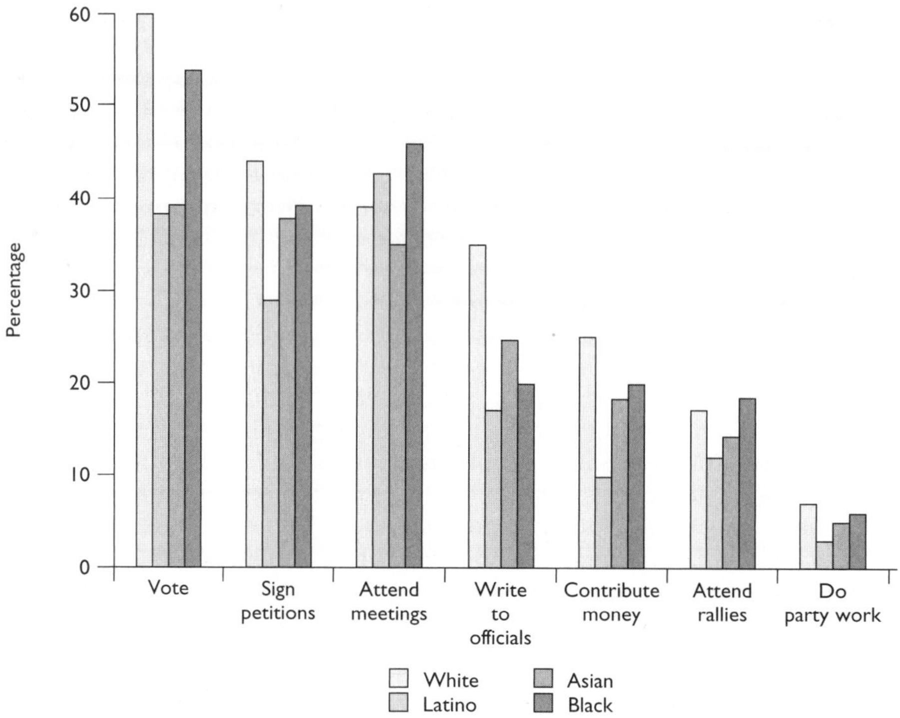

From Public Policy Institute of California, "The Ties That Bind," 2004. Reprinted with permission.

63 percent of people aged 18–24 are registered and only 21 percent vote.[3] All this adds up to a voting electorate that is more conservative than the population as a whole, which means that Republicans can sometimes win statewide elections despite the Democratic edge in registration and that liberal ballot measures rarely pass.

Of course voting is only one form of political participation. Many people sign petitions, attend public meetings, write letters to officials, and contribute money to campaigns. But as Figure 3.1 indicates, the number participating diminishes with each form of engagement, and differences among ethnic groups persist. As a recent study concluded, those who participate most are "white, older, more affluent, homeowners, and more highly educated."[4]

THE CANDIDATES

When we vote, we choose among candidates, but how do candidates come forward in the first place? Some are encouraged to run by political parties or interest groups seeking to advance their causes. Political leaders looking for allies recruit others, although weak political parties make such overtures less common in California than elsewhere. Most California candidates are usually self-starters with an interest in politics who decide to run and then seek support. The rising cost and increasing negativity of campaigns have discouraged some people from running, although wealthy individuals who can fund their own campaigns have appeared as candidates more frequently in recent years. Most candidates start at the bottom of the political ladder, running for school board or city council, and work their way up, building support as they go. Others gain experience as staff members for elected officials, eventually running for their boss's job. Wealthy candidates sometimes skip such apprenticeships and run directly for higher office, but the voters tend to be skeptical about their lack of political experience. Businessman Al Checchi, for example, spent $38 million of his own money running for governor in 1998 but couldn't even win the Democratic party nomination.

Historically, candidates in California have been even less representative of the population than the electorate is. Most have been educated white males of above-average financial means. Only in the 1970s and 1980s did increasing numbers of women, minorities, and gays and lesbians begin to win nominations and elections. All of these groups remain underrepresented in relation to their presence in the electorate.

The 1990s brought change, however. Underrepresented groups grew in strength and organization, and structural changes facilitated their candidacies. A 1990 initiative limited the number of terms that legislators could serve, thus ensuring greater turnover in the state legislature; in addition, the reapportionment decisions after the censuses of 1990 and 2000 resulted in redrawn legislative and Congressional districts that gave minority candidates new opportunities at both levels.

Latinos gained the most from these changes, including a sizable delegation in the legislature. Fabian Nunez, the current speaker of the state assembly, is Latino, as were two of his predecessors. Cruz Bustamante is now serving his second term as lieutenant governor. Latinos have also gained representation at the local level, with more than 20 percent of California's county supervisors, city council members, and mayors being Latino (double their numbers of a decade ago).

Although a smaller minority, African Americans got a foothold in state politics earlier, including the statewide positions of lieutenant governor and superintendent of public instruction. As the longest-serving speaker of the state assembly (1980–1995), Willie Brown was one of California's most powerful politicians for many years. But overall, black representation has shrunk in proportion to other groups. Less than 5 percent of California's county supervisors, city council members, and mayors were African American in 2001.

Asian Americans, however, are the most underrepresented of California's racial minorities, holding just over 3 percent of county supervisor, city council, and mayoral positions. Asian representation in the state legislature has improved recently. Wilma Chan, a Democrat from Oakland and the daughter of Chinese immigrants, has served in the powerful position of majority leader. Meanwhile, Van Tran, a Republican, became the highest-ranking Vietnamese elected official in the United States when he was elected to the state assembly in 2004. In the past, Asian Americans have also won election to statewide offices, including Secretary of State March Fong Eu (1974), U.S. Senator S. I. Hayakawa (1976), and California State Treasurer Matt Fong (1994). However, electing candidates has been difficult for Asian Americans because many are recent immigrants who are not yet rooted in the state's political system and because of cultural and political differences among the Chinese, Japanese, Vietnamese, Filipinos, Koreans, and other Asian American groups.

Women candidates have been more successful. Both of California's U.S. senators are now women, and women have been elected to statewide office in the past, although none are currently serving. A substantial number of women are in the state legislature, however, and 37 percent of California's city council members, mayors, and county supervisors are women.

Lesbians and gays achieved elected office later than any of these groups. Greater bias may be a factor, and in the past, the closeted status of many homosexuals–including candidates and elected officials–weakened organizing efforts and made gay and lesbian successes invisible. More than 40 openly gay and lesbian individuals now hold state or local offices, including a growing number of state legislators. Some, like Senator Sheila Kuehl, a Democrat from Los Angeles, have risen to leadership positions.

Sexism and racism partly explain the underrepresentation of all these groups, but other factors also contribute. Many members of these groups are economically disadvantaged, which makes it hard to participate in politics, let alone to take on the demands of a candidacy. Women, minorities, and gays are usually not plugged in to the network of lobbyists, interest groups, and big donors that funds California's expensive campaigns. Minorities also have difficulty winning support outside their own groups and may alienate their "natural constituencies" in the process. The fact that minorities are less likely to vote than Anglos further reduces their candidates' potential.

CAMPAIGNING CALIFORNIA STYLE

The introduction of primary elections in 1909 shifted the focus of campaigns from political parties to individual candidates. In primary elections, candidates of each party run against one another, and the one who wins the most votes becomes the party's nominee and runs against the nominees of other parties in the general election. Most legislative districts are dominated by one party or the other, so the primary election tends to determine the winner of the general election. But even in statewide elections and competitive legislative districts, California's weakened political parties provide minimal assistance. Political aspirants must raise money, recruit workers, research issues, and plot strategy on their own or with the help of expensive consultants rather than with that of political parties, which contribute little in the way of money or staff. California campaigns thus tend to focus on the personalities of the candidates more than on parties or policies.

Weak parties mean that candidates must promote themselves, so the cost of running for state assembly or senate often exceeds $1 million. Spending on races for the legislature totaled $80.6 million in 1998 and $76.5 million in 2002. Campaigns for statewide offices are even more expensive. The candidates for governor spent a total of $130 million in 1998, $110 million in 2002, and $85 million in the 2003 recall election. The money for campaigns is provided by interest groups, businesses, and wealthy individuals. Much campaign financing is provided by **political action committees (PACs),** which interest groups use to direct money to preferred campaigns. Legislative leaders such as the speaker of the assembly and the president pro tem of the senate raise huge sums from such sources and channel the money to their allies in the legislature, while individual candidates raise money by asking potential contributors directly and through special fund-raising events, which range from coffees and barbecues to banquets and concerts. They also solicit contributions from specific audiences through targeted mailings and the Internet. Some wealthy candidates provide their own funds–Arnold Schwarzenegger provided $8.6 million for his campaign for governor–but most must rely on donors with an interest in the outcome of the election.

Worried about the influence of all this money and turned off by campaign advertising, Californians have approved a series of initiatives aimed at regulating campaign finance. The **Political Reform Act of 1974** required public disclosure of all donors and expenditures. Since then, reformers have tried repeatedly to limit the amount that individuals and groups can contribute, but initiatives approved by the voters have been invalidated by the courts on grounds that they unduly limited free speech. In 2000, voters approved Proposition 34, a legislative initiative setting higher contribution limits than previous measures. Individual contributions are limited to $3,200 for legislative candidates, $5,300 for statewide offices, and $21,200 for governor, while "small contributor committees" can give $6,400 per election to legislative candidates, $10,600 to statewide candidates, and $21,200 to gubernatorial candidates. Proposition 34 also set voluntary spending limits for candidates: $425,000 in the primary and $744,000 in the general election for assembly candidates; $637,000 and $956,000 for senate candidates; and $6,374,000 and $10,624,000 for gubernatorial candidates. Candidates who accept the spending limits have their photo and candidate statements published in the official ballot booklets that go to all voters; candidates who decline the limits are excluded from the booklet. Most candidates comply with the spending limits; those who don't lose the moral high ground to those who do, which often influences voters.

However, the new spending limits have been subverted by **independent expenditures** by PACs or groups specially organized by political consultants in support of candidates. Millions of dollars were spent in this way in the 2004 election. The prison guards' union alone invested $1.3 million in independent expenditures for just eight candidates for state legislature. The only restriction on independent expenditures is that they cannot be coordinated with the campaigns of the candidates they support. Because they are not directly associated with the candidates, "independent" mailings and television ads often feature the most vicious attacks on opponents.

Despite efforts to limit spending, California campaigns have become the most costly in the nation. Other states have avoided California's fate by finding other ways to limit the influence of money in politics, including 13 states that provide public financing for candidate campaigns.

WHAT THE MONEY BUYS

Campaign contributors expect their money to buy immediate access and long-term influence. Candidates deny making specific deals, however, insisting that they and their contributors merely share views on key issues. Millions of dollars flow into candidates' coffers through this murky relationship. Energy and utility companies, for example, gave generously to candidates, including Governor Gray Davis, when the state was shaping and reshaping its energy policies. Revelations about these contributions and others from donors with business before the state added to the problems that resulted in Davis' recall in 2003. Meanwhile, real estate, development, and construction interests were top donors for Arnold Schwarzenegger's campaign to replace Davis.

So much money is needed because California campaigns, whether local or statewide, are highly professionalized. This is nothing new. California publicists Clem Whitaker and Leone Baxter virtually invented modern, mass-media campaigns back in 1934 when they coordinated the media attack on Upton Sinclair, the left-leaning Democratic candidate for governor. To compensate for weak party organizations, candidates hire consultants and management firms to perform a variety of functions, including recruiting workers, raising money, advertising, conducting public opinion polls, and performing virtually all other campaign activities. These specialists understand the workings of California's volatile electorate and use their knowledge to a candidate's benefit.

Television has made campaign management firms indispensable, allowing candidates instant entry into as many homes as there are in the viewing area. It also enables candidates to put their message across at the exact moment of their choosing–between wrestling bouts, during the news or *Oprah,* or just after *Law and Order,* depending on the specific targeted audience. The efficacy of the medium is proved repeatedly when little-known candidates spend big money on television commercials and become major contenders, as Steve Westly did in his 2002 campaign for state controller.

A recent study shows that most California voters judge candidates and issues "mainly by the advertising they see on television, whereas in more compact, less populous states, the proportion drops to two of every three."[5] No wonder television advertising accounts for roughly 80 percent of all spending for statewide races in California. In such a big state, it is the only way to reach the mass of voters, making little-known candidates household names in weeks. At the height of the gubernatorial campaigns, candidates run hundreds of ads a day in California's major media markets. Well-funded initiative campaigns also rely heavily on television advertising. The two sides of the 2002 propositions on Indian gambling, for example, spent a total of $30 million on television ads alone.

Television is too costly for most candidates for legislative and local offices, however. A 30-second prime-time spot can cost over $20,000 in Los Angeles, and because most television stations broadcast to potential audiences much larger than a legislative district, the message is wasted on many viewers. Advertising during the day or on small stations or cable is cheaper, however, and many legislative candidates have turned to these media. Most, however, have found a more efficient way to spend their money: **direct mail.** Computers have revolutionized political mail by enabling campaign strategists to target selected voters with personal messages.

Direct-mail experts develop lists of voters and their characteristics and then send special mailings to people who share particular qualities. In addition to listing voters by party registration and residence, these experts compile data banks that identify various groups, including liberals and conservatives; students, ethnic voters, and retired people; homeowners and renters; union members; feminists and gays; and even those most likely to vote. After the target groups have been identified, campaign strategists can pitch just the right message to them. Conservatives may be told of the candidate's opposition to gay marriage; liberals may be promised action on the environment. For the price of a single 30-second television spot, local or legislative candidates can send multiple mailings to their selected audiences.

Television and direct mail dominate California campaigns because they reach the most voters, but the use of these media is not without problems. Because they are expensive, campaign costs have risen, as has the influence of major donors. Candidates who are unable to raise vast sums of money are usually left at the starting gate. Incumbent officeholders, who are masters at fund-raising and are well connected to major contributors, become invincible. Furthermore, these media are criticized for oversimplifying issues and emphasizing the negative. Television commercials for ballot measures often reduce complicated issues to emotional 30-second spots aimed at uninformed voters. Candidates' ads and mailings indulge in the same oversimplification, often in the form of attacks on their opponents. When the candidates portray each other negatively, voters often feel that they must choose the lesser evil rather than make a decision on the policies and positive traits of the candidates. The voters seem to have grown skeptical of such attacks, yet they are sometimes hard to resist. Campaign consultants, who are usually blamed for the phenomenon, point out that campaigns had a nasty edge even a century ago and that the public pays more attention to negative messages than to positive ones.

Lately, candidates have taken their campaigns to the Internet, setting up websites to provide information and using e-mail to communicate with the media and with supporters. Only two campaigns posted websites during the 1994 election, but more than 300 did so in 2000.[6] Having a website is commonplace now, but the political impact of this new medium is unclear. Whereas television and mail enable the candidates to reach us whether we're interested or not, voters must initiate contact on the Internet, which limits the audience to those who are already interested. Interest groups, however, can use e-mail to send campaign messages to their members, and some candidates have targeted e-mails to particular constituencies, such as Christian conservatives. The Internet can also help candidates recruit volunteers and solicit small donations, which caps on contributions have made more important.

Overall, California's media-oriented campaigns reinforce both the emphasis on candidates' personalities and voter cynicism. Some people blame such campaigns for declining voter turnout. Contemporary campaigns may also depress voter turnout by aiming all their efforts at regular voters and ignoring those who are less likely to vote–often minority voters. Although this is a sensible way to use campaign resources, it is not a way to stimulate democracy.

Some candidates try to revive old-fashioned door-to-door or telephone campaigns and get-out-the-vote drives on election day. Labor union volunteers have become a force in elections in Los Angeles and Santa Clara County, for example, and in 2004, Lori Saldana relied on grassroots volunteers to beat two well-funded opponents and win the Democratic nomination for a San Diego assembly seat–and to win against a well-known Republican in November. Grassroots campaigns have a long and honorable tradition in California, but even in small-scale, local races, they are often up against not only big-money opponents but also the California lifestyle: Few people are at home to be contacted, and those who are may be mistrustful of strangers at their door. For good or ill, candidates need money for their campaigns; those with the most money don't always win, but those with too little rarely even become contenders.

At least that's the way campaigns worked until the recall election of 2003, when the brevity of the campaign and the candidacy of Arnold Schwarzenegger changed everything. State law required a single election, rather than a primary and general election, to be held within 60 to 80 days of the certification of the recall petition. Normally, statewide elections sprawl over at least a year, but when the election was set for October 7, 2003, Governor Davis and the candidates to replace him had just 75 days to make their cases, resulting in the most intense campaign in California history. Candidates who were well known or who could raise funds quickly, like Democratic Lieutenant Governor Cruz Bustamante and Republican Arnold Schwarzenegger, had an instant advantage.

But Schwarzenegger had another advantage. As an internationally famous and glamorous movie star, he attracted massive–and free–media coverage. Schwarzenegger announced his candidacy on Jay Leno's *Tonight Show*, while other candidates called sparsely attended press conferences. His announcement produced intense coverage by CNN and other national news media, which continued through his entire campaign. Where "Arnold" went, the media followed. Schwarzenegger's campaign maximized this coverage with carefully planned, staged events, gaining lots of free television time while avoiding contact with traditional political journalists and their tough questions. Schwarzenegger and Maria Shriver, his wife and a well-known television journalist, appeared on *Oprah;* other candidates were not invited. The movie star candidate also benefited from extensive, if shallow, reporting on shows like *Entertainment Tonight* and *Access Hollywood.*

Although media coverage of the brief campaign was different, some elements of the recall were not. The major candidates relied on television ads and mailings more than ever because time was too short to organize more traditional outreach efforts. Even in so short a campaign, money was still crucial, with over $85 million spent. That means that most of the individuals and interest groups that contribute in other campaigns also gave in the recall. But the recall was also different because interest groups in general were less influential. Indian tribes, labor, and business groups each gave over $10 million to Davis or replacement candidates, but the tribes and unions were on the losing side. Labor and Latino leaders were unable to persuade large numbers of their own voters to oppose the recall and support Bustamante as the replacement. Schwarzenegger succeeded in appealing to these and other traditionally Democratic constituencies, and he balanced the funds going to other candidates with nearly $9 million of his own money and massive free media.[7]

REPORTING ON CALIFORNIA POLITICS

In addition to their role in campaigns, the mass media transmit almost everything that Californians know about politics. They have a profound impact on ideas, issues, and leaders. Until the 1950s, a few family-owned newspapers dominated the media. Then television gave the newspapers some competition while expanding the cumulative clout of the mass media. Before Arnold Schwarzenegger became governor, however, the media–and the public–seemed to have lost interest in news of state politics.

PAPER POLITICS

California's great newspapers were founded in the nineteenth century by ambitious men such as Harrison Gray Otis of the *Los Angeles Times,* William Randolph Hearst of the *San Francisco Examiner,* and James McClatchy of the *Sacramento Bee.* These print-media moguls used their newspapers to boost their communities, their political candidates, and their favored causes. Most were like Otis, an ardent conservative who fought labor unions and pushed for growth while making a fortune in land investments. In the heyday of bosses and machines, his *Los Angeles Times* supported the Southern Pacific Railroad's political machine and condemned Progressive leader Hiram Johnson as a demagogue, as did many other newspapers in the state. Other journalists, however, founded the Lincoln-Roosevelt League and led the campaign for reform.

After reform triumphed over the machine, newspapers continued to play a crucial role in California politics. In Los Angeles, San Francisco, Oakland, San Jose, and San Diego, Republican publishers used the power of the press–on both editorial and news pages–to promote their favorite candidates and causes. They were instrumental in keeping Republicans in office long after the Democrats gained a majority of registered voters.

Change came in the 1970s, when most of California's family-owned newspapers became part of corporate chains. The new managers brought in more professional editors and reporters. News coverage became more objective, and opinion was more consistently confined to the editorial pages. Even the editorials changed, sometimes endorsing Democrats and liberal positions. Meanwhile, the number of daily newspapers published in California declined. At one time, there were hundreds, and every city had several competing with one another. Today, 95 survive, and most cities have just one. Some competition remains, however, as major metropolitan dailies invade one another's turf and as suburban weeklies proliferate. The latter, however, almost never cover state politics.

Many observers worry that newspaper coverage of state politics is becoming almost as superficial as television news. Sports, movie stars, and scandals make the front page; stories on state politics are buried in the newspapers' second sections. Still, every major newspaper in the state maintains a Sacramento bureau, with the *Los Angeles Times* fielding the largest and most respected contingent. And while reporters were once the politicians' pals and the publishers' tools, today's journalists are mostly skilled professionals who seek to tell their stories accurately and objectively.

Besides reporting, newspapers still promote their political favorites through editorial endorsements. Once the personal prerogative of publisher-owners, today these recommendations are made by editorial boards. Newspapers today also try to confine their opinions to their editorial pages and keep their news coverage balanced–unlike the old days. A slight conservative bias persists on the editorial pages, but the pattern is less consistent than it once was, and the influence of these endorsements has declined. Most major newspapers, for example, endorsed neither the recall of Gray Davis nor the election of Arnold Schwarzenegger. Other media, including television and the Internet, have become more important to many people.

TELEVISION POLITICS

Public opinion surveys report that 44 percent of Californians say that they get their news and information about state politics from television, with 35 percent citing newspapers, 10 percent radio, and 4 percent the Internet.[8] But until recently, television coverage of California politics left a lot to be desired.

Before Arnold Schwarzenegger was elected governor, not one of California's television stations, other than those based in Sacramento, operated a news bureau in the state capital. Television news editors avoided state political coverage because they believed that viewers wanted glamorous national stories or local features. In contrast, 20 newspapers employed capital correspondents. The minimal television coverage of state politics–a tiny percentage of newscast time, according to various studies–was mainly drawn from newspaper articles, wire service stories, or events staged by politicians, who struggled to gain any coverage at all. Even candidates for governor had a hard time making local news broadcasts, and most television stations declined to broadcast live candidate debates out of fear of low ratings. Television coverage was so poor that one newspaper declared that it constituted "another California innovation: the all-commercial political campaign."[9] Cynics pointed out that if television doesn't provide news coverage, candidates are forced to buy advertising time–on television. The top two Los Angeles television stations, for example, averaged just 35 seconds a night in political news during the month before California's 2000 presidential primary election–but they received $5.6 million for candidate ads.[10]

AFTER THE RECALL

If previous coverage of state politics was minimal or, in the case of television, virtually nonexistent, the recall election changed all that. Arnold Schwarzenegger brought the cameras back to the campaign trail and to the capitol. Newspaper coverage has also intensified. Television reporters from all over the state–along with their satellite vans–are now regular fixtures in Sacramento, and newspapers are sending more reporters, too. The ongoing budget crisis is partly responsible for the change, especially in the print media, but the main factor is the star power of the governor.

The surge in coverage has led to new contentiousness in Sacramento. While previous governors eagerly solicited press coverage, Schwarzenegger draws it automatically whenever he appears. While previous governors welcomed the press at their events, reporters complain that Schwarzenegger limits their number at his–so they don't overwhelm the other participants, Schwarzenegger's staff explains. As he did during the campaign, Schwarzenegger stages events for the benefit of the cameras, now as a means to communicate his policy positions to the public and to put pressure on the legislature on issues from workers' compensation laws to balancing the budget. He also uses his unprecedented media coverage to campaign for ballot measures that he supports.

Even before the election of Schwarzenegger intensified coverage, reporting of state politics had improved in some ways. Investigative reporting has increased, for example, producing long stories, sometimes in series, that may significantly affect public policy or individual politicians. Election coverage is more balanced, incorporating public opinion polls, computer analyses of campaign finances and voting patterns, and critiques of television commercials. Such reporting doesn't always have a major impact, however. Voters seem to have been unimpressed by the *Los Angeles Times* series about alleged sexual harassment by Arnold Schwarzenegger that ran just before the recall election.

While the traditional print and broadcast media still dominate, more alternatives are becoming available to Californians. Latino newspapers and television and radio stations reach major audiences, especially in Southern California. Talk radio played a crucial role in the recall election, as did the Internet, which offers many sites that focus on politics and provides citizens with direct access to state or local governments (see "Learn More on the World Wide Web" at the end of each chapter). Citizens can even watch their government in action on the California Channel, now available on 114 cable systems.

ELECTIONS, CAMPAIGNS, AND THE MEDIA

A mercurial electorate and weak political parties make the influence of money and media greater in California politics than in other states. Politicians must organize their own campaigns, raise vast sums of money, and then take their cases to the people via direct mail and television. Such campaigns are inevitably personality-oriented, with substantive issues taking a back seat to puff pieces or attacks on opponents. The media provide a check of sorts, but until recently, declining coverage limited its impact. More extensive coverage at the moment is still often superficial, and it is unlikely to continue if the next governor isn't a movie star.

All of this takes us back to the issue of declining voter turnout. The recall election, thanks to its brevity, star power, and media interest, increased turnout, but will that last? Could stronger parties, issue-oriented campaigns, and more news coverage revive voter participation? Maybe, but both campaign consultants and the media say they are already giving the public what it wants.

Notes

1. "Just the Facts: California's Likely Voters," Public Policy Institute of California (www.ppic.org), September 2003.
2. Voter News Service.
3. "Just the Facts: The Age Gap in California Politics," Public Policy Institute of California (www.ppic.org), September 2003.
4. "Participating in Democracy: Civic Engagement in California," Research Brief #86, Public Policy Institute of California (www.ppic.org), April 2004.
5. *New York Times,* October 14, 1994.
6. California Voter Foundation (www.calvoter.com).
7. For a full discussion of the recall campaign, see Larry N. Gerston and Terry Christensen, *Recall! California's Political Earthquake,* Armonk, NY: M. E. Sharpe, 2004.
8. Public Policy Institute of California (www.ppic.org), January 2000.
9. *New York Times,* May 6, 1998.
10. "Dollars vs. Discourse in 2000 Presidential Primaries," Alliance for Better Campaigns (www.bettercampaigns.org).

Learn More on the World Wide Web

Public opinion polls:

Los Angeles Times: www.latimes.com/news/custom/timespoll/

Public Policy Institute of California: www.ppic.org

News about California politics:

A compendium of daily news articles: www.roughandtumble.org.

Elections:

California Journal: www.statenet.com/news/calj/

California Secretary of State: www.ss.ca.gov

California Voter Foundation: www.calvoter.com

Campaign finance: www.campaignfinancesite.org

League of Women Voters: www.ca.lwv.org

Smart Voter: www.smartvoter.org

Learn More at the Library

Mark Baldassare, *A California State of Mind,* Berkeley: University of California Press, or www.ppic.org, 2002. Developments in public opinion.

Gerald C. Lubenow, Ed., *California Votes: The 2002 Governor's Race and the Recall That Made History,* Berkeley, CA: IGS Press, 2004.

Greg Mitchell, *The Campaign of the Century,* New York: Random House, 1992. Upton Sinclair's 1934 campaign for governor.

Chapter 4

INTEREST GROUPS: THE POWER BEHIND THE DOME

Most people belong to one or more **interest groups,** organizations formed to protect and promote the shared objectives of their members. Existing in all shapes and sizes, interest groups range from labor unions, ethnic organizations, and business associations to student unions and automobile clubs.

Interest groups have prospered, proliferated, and become more important than political parties to many Californians. More people pay dues to the California Teachers Association (CTA) or the California Chamber of Commerce, for example, than contribute to the state Republican or Democratic parties. California's political institutions provide a fertile political environment for group power. Weak political parties make candidates dependent on groups for financing, while direct democracy enables groups to make policy. Interest groups also successfully influence legislators in the lobbies beneath the capitol dome. Some observers view these efforts as assisting the legislative process; others see them as manipulating that process. All groups are not equal, however; depending on resources and issues, some are far more successful than others.

THE EVOLUTION OF GROUP POWER IN CALIFORNIA

The astonishing length of California's constitution attests to the historical clout of the state's interest groups. In other states, groups gain advantages such as tax exemptions through state law, which can be changed by the legislature at any time. In California, such protections are often written into the constitution, making them more difficult to alter because constitutional amendments require the approval of the electorate. Among California's constitutionally favored interests are dozens of crops (protecting organized agriculture), trees less than 40 years old (protecting the timber industry), and ships for passengers or freight (protecting the shipping industry). These "safeguards" were not responses to public outcry; interest groups pushed them through for their own benefit.

Different groups have benefited from various eras of California politics. In the early days, the mining industry and ranchers dominated. From about 1870 to 1910, the Southern Pacific Railroad monopolized the state's economy and politics. After the railroad, a diverse group of industries held sway until about 1960. Land development, shipping, and horse racing were prominent early in this period, followed by the automobile and defense industries. Agricultural interests have remained strong through all these periods.

Over the last few decades, the players and the game have changed. Banking and leisure industries now supplement manufacturing, while high-tech industries have taken their place alongside defense and aerospace. Insurance companies, physicians' and attorneys' groups, and other vocation-related associations also lobby state government for favored status. They have been joined by the California Nations Indian Gaming Association, the largest contributor to the 2003 recall campaign. Single-issue groups, such as Gun Owners of California and Mothers Against Drunk Driving (MADD), have also joined the fray, along with evangelical, pro-choice, right-to-life, minority, feminist, and gay and lesbian groups. "Public interest" groups such as Common Cause and the Howard Jarvis Taxpayers Association are also part of the interest group mix.

Group politics in California today is wide open, with every imaginable interest making its claim, facilitated by the state's political system. As a consequence, California politicians often find themselves responding to the demands of interest groups rather than governing them.

THE GROUPS

Interest groups vary in size, resources, and goals. At one extreme, groups that pursue economic benefits tend to have relatively small memberships but a great deal of money, whereas public interest groups often have large memberships but little money. A few, such as the Consumer Attorneys of California (CAC), whose membership consists of trial lawyers, have the dual advantage of being both large and well funded. Others, such as the Consumers for Auto Reliability and Safety, operate on a shoestring.

ECONOMIC GROUPS

Every major corporation in the state, from the Southern Pacific Railroad to Southern California Edison and from the Bank of America to Apple Computer, is represented in Sacramento either by their own lobbyists or by lobbying firms hired to present their cases to policy makers. Often, individual corporations or businesses with similar goals form associations to further their general objectives. These umbrella organizations include the California Manufacturers and Technology Association, the California Business Alliance (for small enterprises), the California Bankers Association, and the California Council for Environmental and Economic Balance (utilities and oil companies). The California Chamber of Commerce alone boasts 12,000 members.

Agribusiness is particularly active because farming depends on the government on issues such as water and pesticides. The giant farming operations maintain their own lobbyists, but various producer groups also form associations. Most of the state's wine makers, for example, are represented by the 782-member Wine Institute. Broader organizations such as the California Farm Bureau, one of the state's most powerful lobby groups, speak for agribusiness in general.

Recently, high-tech industries have asserted their interests on issues ranging from Internet taxation to transportation and education. Organizations such as TechNet, the Silicon Valley Manufacturing Group, and the American Electronics Association have lobbied for regulatory changes, tax relief, relaxed smog emissions rules, and other changes. During the 2003 recall campaign of Governor Gray Davis, Indian gaming interests spent $13 million attempting to keep Davis in office and Arnold Schwarzenegger from winning it–all in all, a poor bet!

PROFESSIONAL ASSOCIATIONS AND UNIONS

Professional associations such as the California Medical Association (CMA), the California Association of Realtors (CAR), and the CAC are among the state's most active groups, and they are regularly among the largest campaign contributors. Other professionals, such as chiropractors, dentists, and general contractors, also maintain active associations. Because all these professionals serve the public, many tend to promote their concerns as broader than self-interest. Their credibility is further enhanced by expertise in their respective fields and by memberships consisting of large numbers of affluent, respected individuals.

Teachers' associations and other public employee organizations fall somewhere between business associations and labor unions. Their members view themselves as professionals but in recent years have increasingly resorted to traditional labor union tactics, such as collective bargaining and strikes. The CTA is the major education group in Sacramento. Other public workers, such as the highway patrol and state university professors, have their own organizations, but the California State Employees Association (CSEA) is the giant among these groups, with more than 137,000 members and the ability to raise large campaign war chests. It regularly ranks with the CMA, CAR, and CAC among the state's top campaign contributors.

Unions have done reasonably well in California, representing 18 percent of the workforce, compared to 13 percent nationwide. Traditional labor unions represent nurses, machinists, carpenters, public utilities employees, and dozens of other occupations. In 2002, many unions worked to persuade the legislature to enact the nation's first paid family leave program, allowing workers to take leave from their jobs for up to six weeks at 55 percent of their salary or a maximum of $728 per week. The new law drew the wrath of the California Chamber of Commerce, which predicted that it would create hardship for businesses.[1]

Perhaps the most visible and controversial union in state politics is the California Correctional Peace Officers Association, which contributed more than $600,000 to the re-election campaign of Governor Gray Davis in 2002 and saw the governor sign a 3-year pay increase of 35 percent in the midst of a huge state budget deficit. The agreement drew tremendous criticism of the union and Davis, adding fuel to the recall accusation that Davis was little more than a tool of major contributors.[2] In 2004, Governor Arnold Schwarzenegger renegotiated the contract and won a 6-month delay in the pay raises, but he achieved only about one third of the savings he targeted.

DEMOGRAPHIC GROUPS

A set of groups that depends more on membership than on money can be described as **demographic groups.** Based on characteristics that distinguish their members from other segments of the population, such as their ethnicity, gender, or age, such groups usually have an interest in overcoming discrimination. Most racial and ethnic organizations fall into this category.

Virtually all of California's minorities have organizations to speak for them. One of the earliest of these was the Colored Convention, which fought for the rights of blacks in California in the nineteenth century. Today, several such groups advocate for African Americans, Asians, and Native Americans. The United Farm Workers (UFW), GI Forum, Mexican American Legal Defense Fund (MALDEF), and Mexican American Political Association (MAPA) represent Latinos.

The National Organization for Women (NOW) and National Women's Political Caucus (NWPC) actively support women candidates and feminist causes. Both groups have organized better at the local level than at the state level, however. The same may be said of gays and lesbians, except when disputing what were viewed as antigay initiatives in 1978, 1986, 1988, and 2000.

Age groups play a smaller part in state politics, but with an aging population heavily dependent on public services, organizations such as the American Association of Retired Persons (AARP), with no less than 3 million members, have achieved a higher profile in state politics, particularly on health-care issues.

All of these groups, whether based on race, age, gender, or sexual orientation, derive their strength almost exclusively from the size of their memberships. Racial, ethnic, feminist, and gay and lesbian organizations, however, have also proved capable of raising big money for selected candidates and causes.

SINGLE-ISSUE GROUPS

The groups discussed so far tend to have broad bases and to deal with a wide range of issues. Another type of interest group operates with a broad base of support for the resolution of narrow issues. **Single-issue groups** push for a specific question to be decided on specific terms. They support only candidates who agree with their particular position on an issue. The California Abortion Rights Action League (CARAL), for example, endorses only candidates who support abortion (pro-choice), whereas antiabortion (or pro-life) groups work only for candidates on the opposite side. Likewise, the Howard Jarvis Taxpayers Association evaluates candidates and ballot propositions solely in terms of whether they meet the association's objective of no unnecessary taxes and no wasteful government spending.

Each of these groups exercises power on occasion, but the reluctance to compromise limits their effectiveness in the give-and-take of state politics. Nevertheless, a group's ability to deliver a solid bloc of voters can affect the outcome of a close election and thus enhance its clout, at least on a temporary basis. In recent elections, groups as varied as the National Rifle Association (NRA), Christian conservatives, and taxpayers' associations have claimed such an impact.

PUBLIC INTEREST GROUPS

Although virtually all organized interests claim to speak for the broader public interest, some groups clearly seek no private gain and thus more correctly claim to be **public interest groups.** Consumer groups, for example, campaign for the public interest in the marketplace. Some such groups have pushed for insurance reform, whereas others, such as Toward Utility Rate Normalization, monitor rate requests by the utilities before the state Public Utilities Commission. Environmental organizations such as the Sierra Club and Friends of the Earth have been particularly active in California on issues such as water management, offshore oil drilling, air pollution, transportation, and pesticide use. Land use is another important concern of these groups, both for private development in sensitive areas and for public lands, which comprise half the state. A recent survey found that one in nine Californians claims to belong to an environmental group.[3]

Other public interest groups, such as California Public Interest Research Group, Common Cause, and the League of Women Voters, focus on governmental reform. These groups have been involved in several efforts to reform campaign finance in California.

A final type of public interest group isn't really a group at all: local governments. Cities, school districts, special districts, and counties all lobby the state government, on whose funds they depend heavily, through the League of California Cities, the California School Boards Association, and the California State Association of Counties (CSAC). Dozens of cities and counties employ their own lobbyists in Sacramento, as do other governmental agencies. They also endorse ballot measures that affect their interests and, on rare occasions, even sponsor initiatives, but unlike other groups, cities and counties cannot make campaign contributions or organize their constituents.

TECHNIQUES AND TARGETS: INTEREST GROUPS AT WORK

The goal of interest groups is to influence public policy. To do this, they must persuade policy makers. The legislature, the executive branch, the courts, and sometimes the people are thus the targets of the various techniques these groups may use.

LOBBYING

The term **lobbying** refers to the activity that once went on in the lobbies outside the legislative chambers. Group advocates would buttonhole legislators on their way in or out and make their cases. This still goes on in the lobbies and hallways of the capitol, as well as in nearby bars and restaurants and wherever else policy makers congregate.

Until the 1950s, lobbying was a crude and disreputable activity. Lobbyists lavished food, drink, gifts, and money on legislators. Artie Samish, the prototype for modern lobbyists, perfected the craft first by learning about state government as a legislative staffer and then by representing breweries, unions, racetracks, banks, railroads, tobacco corporations, and the chemical industry. He bestowed money on legislative allies and used his knowledge of their personal lives to influence them. "On matters that affect his clients," Governor Earl Warren once said, "Artie unquestionably has more power than the governor."[4] Samish fell from power, however, after his 1953 conviction for income tax evasion.

Today's lobbyists, like Samish, are experts on the legislative process. Many have served as legislators or staff members. They focus on **legislative committees** and leaders, lobbying the full legislature only as a last resort. Unlike their predecessors, lobbyists must be well informed to be persuasive with today's more sophisticated legislators. They still use money, but less crudely than Samish, instead strategically contributing to campaigns. Legislators and lobbyists alike assert that contributions buy access, not votes, but the tie between money and access can be powerful in its own right. In the words of a former lobbyist for the California Medical Association, money is "the single most powerful engine driving public policy. . . ."[5] All of this makes lobbying not only a highly specialized profession but also an expensive activity. In fact, during 2003, lobby firms were paid about $228,000,000 to influence the legislative process–that's about $1.9 million per legislator![6]

Between 1977 and 2003, the number of registered lobbyists in Sacramento nearly doubled from 582 to 1,078, including about two dozen former legislators. Most represent a particular business, union, organization, or group. **Contract lobbyists,** who work for several clients simultaneously, are on the rise, however. Kahl/Pownall Advocates, for example, represents the Western States Petroleum Association, insurance companies, Citigroup, General Electric, and Pacific Telesis. With clients paying more than $9.2 million, they were California's top lobbying firm during 2001–2002 (Table 4.1).

Whether contract or specialized, more and more lobbyists make a career of their professions, accruing vast knowledge and experience. These long-term professionals became even more powerful when term limits eliminated senior legislators with countervailing knowledge, although some lobbyists complain that term limits mean they must constantly reestablish their credibility with new decision makers. One prominent lobbyist, however, explains his lack of concern about term limits or other reforms: "Whatever your rules are, I'm going to win," he says.[7]

Not all lobbying is done by professionals. Some groups can't afford to hire a lobbyist, so they rely on their members instead. Even groups with professional help use their members on occasion to show elected officials

TABLE 4.1

CALIFORNIA'S FIVE LARGEST LOBBY ORGANIZATIONS, 2001–2002

COMPANY	AMOUNT COLLECTED
Kahl/Pownall Advocates	$9.2 million
Platinum Advisors	$7.4 million
Nielsen, Merksamer, Parrinello, Mueller & Naylor	$7.4 million
Aaron Read & Associates	$5.3 million
Rose & Kindel	$5.3 million

the breadth of their support. Usually, this sort of lobbying is conducted by individuals who reside in the districts of targeted legislators, although groups sometimes lobby *en masse,* busing members to the capitol for demonstrations or concurrent lobbying of many elected officials.

Such grassroots efforts by nonprofessionals have special credibility with legislators, but well-financed groups have learned to mimic grassroots groups by forming front groups or "Astroturf" organizations that conceal their real interests. Prison guards, for example, backed Crime Victims United, and the building industry formed Californians for Schools.

Although most lobbying is focused on the legislature, knowledgeable professionals also target the executive branch, from the governor down to the bureaucracy. The governor not only proposes the budget but also must respond to thousands of bills that await his or her approval or rejection. The bureaucracy must interpret new laws and make future recommendations to the governor. These responsibilities do not escape the attention of astute interest groups.

Lately, the public has become a target of lobbying, too. In media-addicted California, groups have begun making their cases through newspaper and television advertising between elections. Health care, education, Indian gaming, and other issues have been subjects of costly media campaigns.

CAMPAIGN SUPPORT

Most groups also try to further their cause by helping sympathetic candidates win election and re-election. Groups with limited financial resources do so by providing volunteers to go door-to-door or to serve as phone-bank callers for candidates. Labor unions in Los Angeles and San Jose have been particularly successful at electing candidates whom they endorse; agricultural organizations in the Central Valley have enjoyed similar successes.

Groups with greater resources make generous campaign contributions. Sometimes such contributions appear to get the groups what they want. Tobacco companies, for example, dramatically increased their campaign contributions to legislators and legislative candidates between 1997 and 2002, adding nearly $10 million. In 2003, the legislature passed and Governor Davis signed two laws shielding the industry from massive damage awards.[8] But sometimes groups fail, no matter how much they contribute. In 2002, banks, insurance companies, and similar interests contributed more than $20 million in campaign contributions to defeat a bill by state Senator Jackie Speier aimed at protecting the financial privacy of consumers.[9] Facing a similar outcome in 2003, Speier organized an initiative campaign and quickly collected 600,000 signatures; the moneyed interests retreated, and Speier's bill (SB1) was signed into law by Governor Davis. Different groups came out winners and losers in the 2003 recall election, too. Indian gaming interests spent $13 million opposing the recall, while business interests spent an equal amount in support of the recall and the election of Arnold Schwarzenegger.

Campaign contributors claim that their money merely buys them access to decision makers, but the press and the public often suspect a more conspiratorial process, and evidence of money-for-vote trades has emerged in recent years. FBI agents posing as businessmen asked legislators for favors in exchange for campaign contributions, resulting in the 1994 convictions of 14 people, including 5 legislators. Their trials revealed the extent to which legislators hustle lobbyists for contributions. More recently, California's elected insurance commissioner was forced to resign when it was discovered that he let insurance companies accused of wrongdoing avoid big fines by giving smaller amounts to foundations that subsequently spent the money on polls, ads featuring the commissioner, and other activities. As a result of these scandals, politicians and contributors probably exercise greater caution, but the high cost of campaigning in California means that candidates continue to ask and lobbyists and interest groups continue to give.

LITIGATION

Litigation is an option when a group questions the legality of legislation, and in recent years, many groups have turned to the courts for a final interpretation of the law. Groups have challenged state laws in court, such as in 2003 when the California Medical Association successfully sued to keep the legislature from reducing Medi-Cal payments by 5 percent, or $300 million. Opponents have also raised legal challenges to several successful ballot measures, such as those on immigration, affirmative action, campaign finance, and bilingual education, hoping that the initiatives would be declared unconstitutional. Even if a group loses its case, it may delay the implementation of a new law or at least establish a principle for debate in the future. In 2001, MALDEF challenged the legislature's redistricting plan, claiming underrepresentation of Latinos. Although MALDEF lost the case, the tactic kept the issue on the public agenda.

DIRECT DEMOCRACY

Hiram Johnson championed the initiative in 1911 "to make every man [sic] his own legislature," but today only broad-based or well-financed groups have the resources to collect the necessary signatures or to pay for expensive campaigns. Direct democracy gives interest groups the opportunity to make policy themselves by promoting their proposals through initiatives and referenda.

Every initiative on the ballot represents major organizing efforts and spending by interest groups. In 1998, for example, tribal supporters of gambling on Indian lands spent $10 million qualifying an initiative for the ballot in just 30 days–the most expensive petition campaign in history. The subsequent campaign on the proposition itself also broke records, with the two sides spending a total of $96 million. The voters ultimately approved the initiative.

Recall is also sometimes used by interest groups, usually to remove local elected officials. Teachers' unions, conservative Christians, and minority groups have conducted recall campaigns against school trustees, for example. These efforts pale in comparison, however, to the recall effort against Gray Davis. The People's Advocate, a conservative antitax group, was among the leading forces early in the recall effort. During the campaign, groups ranging from the Howard Jarvis Taxpayers Association to the League of Conservation Voters weighed in on the issue.

REGULATING GROUPS

Free spending by interest groups and allegations of corruption led to Proposition 9, the **Political Reform Act of 1974**, an initiative sponsored by Common Cause. Overwhelmingly approved by the voters, the law requires politicians to report their assets, disclose contributions, and declare how they spend campaign funds. Other provisions compel lobbyists to register with the secretary of state, file quarterly reports on their campaign-related activities, and reveal the beneficiaries of their donations. The measure also established the **Fair Political Practices Commission (FPPC),** an independent regulatory body, to monitor these activities. When the commission finds incomplete or inaccurate reporting, it may fine the violator. Of greater concern than the financial penalty, however, is the bad press for those who incur the commission's reprimand. The voters approved new constraints in 1996, when they enacted strict limits on interest groups' practice of rewarding supportive legislators with travel and generous fees for speeches. However, this legislation was soon challenged, creating an atmosphere of uncertainty. In 2000, voters approved yet another initiative, Proposition 34, which placed new constraints on political action committees and attempted to limit contributions to political campaigns.

MEASURING GROUP CLOUT: MONEY, NUMBERS, AND CREDIBILITY

Campaign regulations are generally intended to reduce the disproportionate influence of moneyed interests in state politics, but economic groups still have the advantage. Their money makes the full panoply of group tactics available to them and gives them the staying power to outlast the enthusiasm and energy of grassroots groups. Public interest groups and demographic groups, however, gain strength from numbers, credibility, and motives other than self-interest. Occasionally, they prevail, such as in 1998, when children's and health groups overcame a campaign disadvantage of $30 million to $10 million to pass Proposition 10, a cigarette tax dedicated to children's health programs.

How powerful are interest groups and their lobbyists? It's hard to tell, but an informal survey of 12 first-time legislators reported that lobbyists wrote 70 percent of the bills they proposed.[10] Whatever the balance among groups, they are central to California politics. Besides California's weak political parties and its opportunities for direct democracy, California's diversity, with so many groups clamoring for favor, makes that inevitable.

Notes

1. *California Business Issues, 2004,* California Chamber of Commerce, Sacramento California, p. 77.
2. See Larry N. Gerston and Terry Christensen, *Recall! California's Political Earthquake,* Armonk, NY: M. E. Sharpe, 2004, p. 22.
3. Public Policy Institute of California (www.ppic.org), *Statewide Survey,* June 2000.
4. Quoted in Lester Velie, "The Secret Boss of California," *Collier's,* August 13, 1949, p. 13.
5. "Legislature for Sale," *San Jose Mercury News,* January 8, 1995, p. 20A.
6. "Sacramento's Top Lobbyists," *California Journal,* November 2003, p. 42.
7. Douglas Foster, "The Lame Duck State," *Harper's,* February 1994.
8. See "California: The Campaign Contributions and Lobbying Expenditures of the Tobacco Industry and Its Allies," Common Cause Education Fund, October 2002, and "How Big Tobacco Got Its Way in California," *Los Angeles Times,* September 14, 2003, pp. C1, C5.
9. "$20 million tab to a defeat a privacy bill," *San Francisco Chronicle,* September 7, 2002, pp. A1, A11.
10. See note 7, p. 44.

Learn More on the World Wide Web

Lobbying and campaign spending:

www.ss.ca.gov

www.calvoter.org

Interest groups:

California Association of Realtors (CAR): www.car.org

California Chamber of Commerce: www.calchamber.com

California Common Cause: www.commoncause.org/states/california

California Labor Federation: www.calaborfed.org

The Howard Jarvis Tax Association: www.hjta.org

Latino Issues Forum: www.lif.org

League of Women Voters: www.ca.lwv.org

Sierra Club: www.sierraclub.org/chapters/ca

Learn More at the Library

Political Action Handbook, California Journal, Fifth Edition, 1995.

Arthur H. Samish and Bob Thomas, *The Secret Boss of California*, New York: Crown, 1971.

Dan Walters and Jay Michael, *The Third House*, Berkeley, CA: Berkeley Public Policy Press, 2002.

CHAPTER 5

THE LEGISLATURE: THE PERILS OF POLICY MAKING

Thousands of bills are introduced in the California legislature every year. Some are trivial, such as establishing rules for tattoo-removal equipment or determining the official ghost town of the state. But along with deciding lightweight issues, the legislature is responsible for solving the state's thorniest problems, such as underfunded public education, inadequate revenues, and a decaying infrastructure. Each year the members write laws and, along with the governor, determine the budget and define services and programs. As the center of such power, the legislature is a natural target of public scrutiny, and criticism of it is understandable. Less understandable, however, is its inability to resolve big issues.

For the last 15 years, California governors and the legislature have tangled on a regular basis. Rarely has the annual budget, perhaps the most pressing of all legislative responsibilities, been enacted on schedule, leading to great tension between the two branches. In addition, the legislature has suffered internally due to political–and philosophical–battles between the largely liberal Democratic majority and the potent conservative Republican minority. Then there's the question of priorities. Some observers have wondered in recent years how it is that the legislature could immerse itself in issues such as the proposed prohibition of foie gras (duck liver), yet seemingly avoid questions like tax reform and gay marriage.[1] It's no wonder that a 2004 public opinion survey found people critical of the state legislature by a margin of nearly two to one, only slightly higher than the dark days just before the recall of then-Governor Gray Davis.[2]

Still, the legislature was established as the state institution most directly linking the people with their government. The question is, does it still do its job in the twenty-first century?

THE MAKING AND UNMAKING OF A MODEL LEGISLATURE

California's first constitution provided a **bicameral** (two-house) **legislature** similar to the U.S. Congress. When the constitution was revised in 1879, the senate was fixed at 40 members serving 4-year terms (with half the body elected every 2 years), and the assembly was set at 80 members serving 2-year terms.

Legislative districts for both houses were originally determined by population, with members representing approximately equal numbers of people. Voters changed the system in 1926 through a constitutional amendment that organized the legislature like the U.S. Congress. Assembly members, like their counterparts in the U.S. House of Representatives, were elected on the basis of population, and senators were elected by county in the same way that each state has two U.S. senators.[3] The large number of counties north of the Tehachapi Mountains permitted the north to dominate the state senate despite Southern California's growth. By 1965, 21 of the 40 state senators in California represented 10 percent of the population; Los Angeles County, home to 35 percent of the state's residents, had but a single state senator.

THE SHIFT TOWARD PROFESSIONALISM

Legislative leadership and organization didn't matter much during the Southern Pacific machine-dominated years (see Chapters 1 and 2). The office of speaker of the assembly, prized today, was passed almost casually from one member to another with each new 2-year session. Even after the railroad's demise as the dominant political force, the legislature remained vulnerable to numerous powerful interest groups. But the transformation of California pushed the legislature to modernize, too.

The legislature's composition changed radically after the U.S. Supreme Court handed down its ***Reynolds v. Sims*** decision in 1964, which ordered all states to organize the upper house of their legislature by population rather than by county or territory. The shift increased urban and southern representation dramatically, with rural and northern representation experiencing a corresponding decline. The new leaders were younger, better educated, and more ideological, and more of them were members of racial minorities.

In 1966, voters approved a ballot proposition to create a full-time legislature with full-time salaries. Until then, the part-time legislature met for no more than 120 days every other year to consider general laws; 2-year state budgets were enacted during the in-between years. Since 1967, however, the legislature has met on an average of more than 200 days per year, with salaries to match. As of 2004, their base salary was

$99,000 (highest among the 50 states); perks pushed annual incomes near $130,000.[4]

REAPPORTIONMENT: KEEPING AND LOSING CONTROL

Based on a 2005 state population of 37,000,000, each assembly district has about 462,500 residents; each senate district has about 925,000. Over time, district sizes change due to growth and population movements, leading some districts to become much larger than others. So that districts stay relatively equal in size, the legislature realigns assembly, senate, and U.S. congressional districts after each national census, which is conducted every 10 years. This seemingly straightforward process, called **reapportionment,** has become intensely political in California.

Until 1991, reapportionment occurred after negotiations between the majority and minority parties. With Republican Governor Pete Wilson taking office alongside a legislature with Democratic majorities, however, the process changed. Wilson vetoed a plan that he viewed as overly favorable to the Democratic party. He then appointed a reapportionment commission to draw new district lines, the results of which appeared to aid Republicans. Ultimately, the reapportionment plan was approved by the state supreme court. Despite Wilson's efforts, the legislature remained in Democratic hands for all but 2 years of the next decade. The state congressional delegation also continued with a Democratic majority, except for a 26–26 tie during the 1995–1996 period.

The 2001 reapportionment took place under different circumstances. With the Democrats controlling both the executive and legislative branches, the redistricting effort went smoothly. This time, Democrats and Republicans agreed on a plan that, while providing equal numbers in each district, basically preserved the status quo. However, because the 2001 plan packed strong Democratic or Republican majorities into almost every district, the partisan division of legislature after the 2002 election was almost identical to the pattern before the election. As a result, some complain that the real elections now take place in one-sided party primaries, rather than in competitive November election contests.[5]

NEW PLAYERS, NEW RULES

Reapportionment, the change from part-time to full-time legislators, and higher salaries transformed the legislature. The new framework attracted better-educated and more professional individuals and also made elected office more feasible for women and minorities. Thus, in 2005 the assembly included 25 women, 18 Latinos, 4 African Americans, 5 Asians, and 3 gay members; the senate included 12 women, 9 Latinos, 2 African Americans, and 3 gay members (Figure 5.1). Women, the largest bloc, now constitute more than 30 percent of the legislature's members.

FIGURE 5.1

Women and Minorities in the California Legislature, 1975–2006

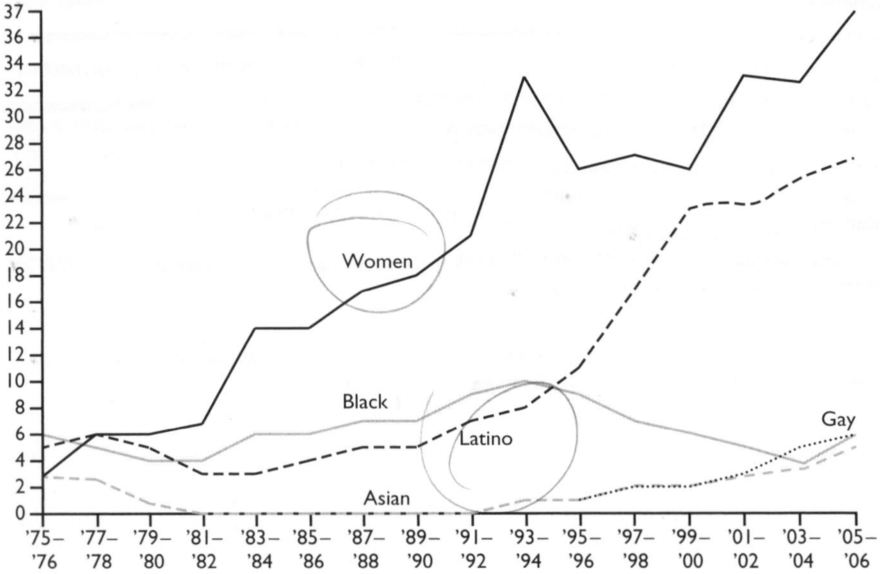

Compiled from *The California Almanac of Government and Politics;* clerks of the assembly and senate.

Despite greater diversity, the legislature has narrowed in terms of vocational backgrounds. During the 1980s, legislative aspirants from the business world were flanked by large numbers of lawyers, local activists, educators, and former legislative aides. But increasingly, the "business candidate" has emerged as the dominant category of self-description. During the 1990s, about half of all legislative candidates on the ballot listed some form of business as their occupations. Beginning in the late 1990s, large numbers of people from city and county elected posts also took seats in the legislature.[6]

Much of the legislature's new look stems from rising voter antipathy toward incumbents and the near certainty of their perpetual re-election. Voter anger peaked in 1990 with the passage of **Proposition 140,** a term-limit initiative for legislators and statewide elected officials. To guarantee periodic turnover, this measure limited elected executive branch officers and state senators to two 4-year terms and assembly members to three 2-year terms; it also cut the legislature's operating budget (and thus its staff) by 38 percent. Clearly, California voters thought their legislature had become too professional for its own good.

TERM LIMITS IN PERSPECTIVE

When term-limit advocates proposed the concept, they envisioned a "turnstile" type of legislature whose members would be in office for relatively short periods. This system was designed to guarantee new faces, reduce the influence of money, and enhance fresh ideas. Of the 17 states with term-limit legislation in place, California is tied with Arkansas and Michigan for the strictest conditions in the nation.

Some objectives associated with term limits have been met, while others show no sign of coming to pass. New faces have certainly appeared, particularly women and minorities, but in many cases, legislators have simply jumped from one house to the other. Although the flow of money into campaign coffers has been slowed, the overall costs of campaigning continue to set new records. As for fresh ideas, the jury is still out. Ironically, a study of the first complete class of assembly members under term limits in 1996 showed remarkable similarity between the new legislators and the so-called professionals who dominated before Proposition 140.[7]

Whereas term limits ensure brief periods of legislative service, there are no limits on the "service" of bureaucrats and lobbyists. Because of their knowledge, nonelected individuals have become increasingly important in shaping the legislative environment. Meanwhile, leadership positions in the legislature, although not as lightly regarded as a century ago, no longer carry the clout that once made the legislature an orderly and effective counterweight to the executive branch.

Nationwide, the term-limit movement seems to be abating. Mississippi voters rejected the concept in 1999. In 2002, the Idaho legislature removed term limits, and the Oregon state supreme court found the state law on term limits unconstitutional. Nevertheless, in March 2002, California voters rejected Proposition 45, a ballot proposition that would have preserved term limits while enabling legislators to add 4 years. For those seeking a career in public office, term limits remain a death knell.

LEADERS AND FOLLOWERS

Although the two houses share lawmaking responsibilities, they function differently. The assembly is more hierarchical, with the **speaker of the assembly** clearly in charge. The speaker controls the flow of legislation, committee chairs and assignments, and vast campaign funds. The number of standing, or topical, committees varies each term with the speaker's organization. For example, there were 29 such committees in the assembly during 2003–2004, equaling the number of the previous session. Some committees are far more important than others, so the speaker's friendship is of great value to a legislator. The speaker also carries favor with the governor, especially if the two work well together. The results can be stunning, as in 2000 when then-Speaker Bob Hertzberg requested $38 million in "special project" funds from the state budget for his district–13 percent of the entire legislature's request–and received virtually everything he sought.

By tradition, the party with a majority in the assembly chooses the speaker in a closed meeting, or caucus. A vote is then taken by the full assembly, with the choice already known to all. The minority party selects its leader in a similar fashion. Majority and minority floor leaders, as well as their whips (assistants), provide further support for the legislative officers. With solid majorities almost consistently since 1959 (Table 5.1), the Democrats have controlled the speakership for all but 4 years during the last 4 decades.

The last dominant speaker, Democrat Willie Brown of San Francisco, held the position from 1980 until 1995–a record. But term limits and a national trend in 1994 briefly swept the Republicans back into power and the speakership. Republican rule lasted through 1996, when the Democrats captured a majority and selected Cruz Bustamante of Fresno as the assembly's first Latino speaker. This time, term limits, not legislative turnover, dictated the length of his stay. Term limits forced Bustamante to yield the speakership to fellow Democrat Antonio Villaraigosa in 1998,

TABLE 5.1

POLITICAL PARTIES IN THE STATE LEGISLATURE, 1975–2006

	SENATE			ASSEMBLY	
LEGISLATIVE SESSION	DEMOCRATS	REPUBLICANS	INDEPENDENTS	DEMOCRATS	REPUBLICANS
1975–1976	25	15		55	25
1977–1978	26	14		57	23
1979–1980	25	15		50	30
1981–1982	23	17		48	32
1983–1984	25	14	1	48	32
1985–1986	25	15		47	33
1987–1988	24	15	1	44	36
1989–1990	24	15	1	47	33
1991–1992	27	12	2	47	33
1993–1994	23	15	2	49	31
1995–1996	21	17	2	39	41
1997–1998	22	17	1	42	38
1999–2000	25	15		48	32
2001–2002	26	14		50	30
2003–2004	25	15		48	32
2005–2006	25	15		48	32

returning power to Southern California for the first time since 1974. Southern California's dominance has continued ever since, with the election of Bob Hertzberg in 2000, Herb Wesson in 2001, and Fabian Nunez in 2004.

Traditionally, the senate has emphasized collegiality and cooperation over strong leadership, strict rules, and tight organization. However, both the senate hierarchy and key committees have assumed more partisan overtones over the last two decades. The most powerful member is the **president pro tem,** who, like the speaker, is elected by the majority party after each general election. The minority party also elects its leader at that time. The key to senate power lies within the five-member **Rules Committee,** which is chaired by the president pro tem and controls all other committee assignments and the flow of legislation. In 2003–2004, the senate had 25 standing committees, the same number as the previous few years.

Senate partisanship increased in 1980, when Los Angeles Democrat David Roberti was chosen as president pro tem. As chair of the Rules Committee, Roberti doubled the size of the committee's staff; he also used his office to raise and dispense large sums to grateful fellow Democrats. In the process, Roberti made the post of president pro tem more like that of the assembly speaker. Term limits forced Roberti to step down in 1994. He was replaced by fellow Democrat Bill Lockyer of Hayward, one of the last pre–Proposition 140 legislators, until term limits forced him to move on in 1998. Democrat John Burton of San Francisco, previously an assembly member for nearly 20 years, replaced Lockyer. Because of his experience, many observers viewed him as the legislature's most formidable leader, despite the assembly speaker's traditionally dominant role. Burton was succeeded in 2005 by Democratic majority leader Don Perata, his right-hand man. Perata's selection assured northern Californians representation among the legislative leadership.

STAFFING THE PROFESSIONAL LEGISLATURE

The evolution of the legislature into a full-time body was accompanied by a major expansion of its support staff. In 1990, the number of legislative assistants totaled 2,400—a far cry from the 485 employed by the last part-time legislature in 1966. Reductions from Proposition 140 pared the number of staffers to about 1,750, although increases in the state's population have led to a slow increase in the number of positions. Today about 2,500 staffers work for the legislature. Those in the capital usually concentrate on pending legislation, whereas district staffers spend much of their time on constituents' problems. The efforts of these staffers help each legislator to remain in good standing with his or her district.

Legislators spend much of their time in committees, the heart of the legislative process. Most committees cover specialized policy areas, such as education or natural resources. A few, such as the senate and assembly

Rules Committees, deal with procedures and internal organization. Each committee employs staff consultants who are both experts on the committee's subject area and politically astute individuals–important attributes because they serve at the pleasure of the committee chair. Besides the traditional committees, staffers assist some 110 select committees (35 in the senate and 75 in the assembly, as of 2004) and 10 joint committees that research narrow issues, coordinate two-house policy efforts, and oversee previously enacted legislation.

Another staff group is even more political. Employed by the Democratic and Republican caucuses and answering to the party leaders in the senate and assembly, these assistants are supposed to deal with possible legislation. However, their real activities usually center on advancing the interests of their party.

In addition to personal, committee, and leadership staffers, legislators have created neutral support agencies. With a staff of 53, the **legislative analyst** (a position created in 1941) provides fiscal expertise, reviewing the annual budget and assessing programs that affect the state's coffers. The **legislative counsel** (created in 1913) employs about 80 attorneys to draft bills for legislators and determine their potential impact on existing legislation. The **state auditor** (created in 1955) assists the legislature by periodically reviewing ongoing programs.

Historically, staffing has enhanced the legislature's professionalism. Yet some staffers, especially those who work for the legislative leaders, clearly spend more time on partisan politics than on legislation. Many have used their positions as apprenticeships to gain knowledge, skills, and contacts for their own campaign efforts. All this, critics point out, is funded by the taxpayers. Defenders of the system counter that this staffing system helps compensate for weak party organizations.

HOW A BILL BECOMES A LAW

The legislature passes laws; it also proposes constitutional amendments, which may be submitted for voter approval after they receive absolute two-thirds majority votes in both houses (the votes of two thirds of the full membership–that is, 27 votes in the senate and 54 in the assembly). The same absolute two-thirds majority votes are required for the legislature to offer bond measures–money borrowed for long-term, expensive state projects. Proposed bond measures must then obtain majority votes at the next election before becoming law.

Most of the legislature's energy, however, is spent on lawmaking. Absolute majorities–21 votes in the senate and 41 votes in the assembly–are required to pass basic laws intended to take effect the following January, but absolute two-thirds votes in both houses are required for appropriations, urgency measures (those that become law immediately upon the governor's signature), and overrides of the governor's veto. The process, however, is far from simple.

THE FORMAL PROCESS

The legislative process begins when the assembly member or senator sponsoring a bill gives the clerk of the chamber a copy, which is recorded and numbered (Figure 5.2). The bill then undergoes three readings and several hearings before it is sent to the other house, where the process is repeated. The first reading simply acknowledges the bill's submission. Typically, a bill is assigned to two or three committees for careful scrutiny by members who are experts in that bill's subject area.

Depending on the bill's origin, either the senate Rules Committee or the assembly Rules Committee decides on the route of the bill. The chairs of these important committees can also affect a bill's fate by sending it to "friendly" or "hostile" committees and by assigning it a favorable or unfavorable route. More than half of all bills die in committee.

More than 6,000 bills are introduced during each 2-year session, with assembly members limited to 50 proposals and senators limited to 65. With such volume, legislative committees are essential to getting laws passed. They hold hearings, debate, and eventually vote on each bill delegated to them. Most committees deal in narrow areas, but a few, such as the senate Finance Committee and the assembly Ways and Means Committee, focus on the collection and distribution of funds and thus enjoy clout that goes beyond any one policy area.

At the conclusion of its hearings, a committee can kill a bill, release it without recommendation, or approve it with a "do pass" proposal. It may also recommend approval contingent on certain changes or amendments. Only when a bill receives a positive recommendation from all of the committees in a house is it likely to get a second reading by the full legislative body. At this stage, the house considers additional amendments. After all proposed revisions have been discussed, the bill is printed in its final form and presented to the full house for a third reading. After further debate on the entire bill, a vote is taken.

If approved, the bill goes to the other house, where the process starts anew. Again, the bill may die anywhere along the perilous legislative path. If the two houses pass different versions of the same bill, the versions must be reconciled by a **conference committee.** Senate members are appointed by the Rules Committee; assembly members are chosen by the speaker. If the conference committee agrees on a single version and if both houses approve it by the required margins, the bill goes to the governor for his or her approval. Otherwise, the proposed legislation is dead.

Usually, a bill becomes law if the governor signs it or takes no action within 12 days. However, if it was passed immediately before a session's

FIGURE 5.2
HOW A BILL BECOMES A LAW

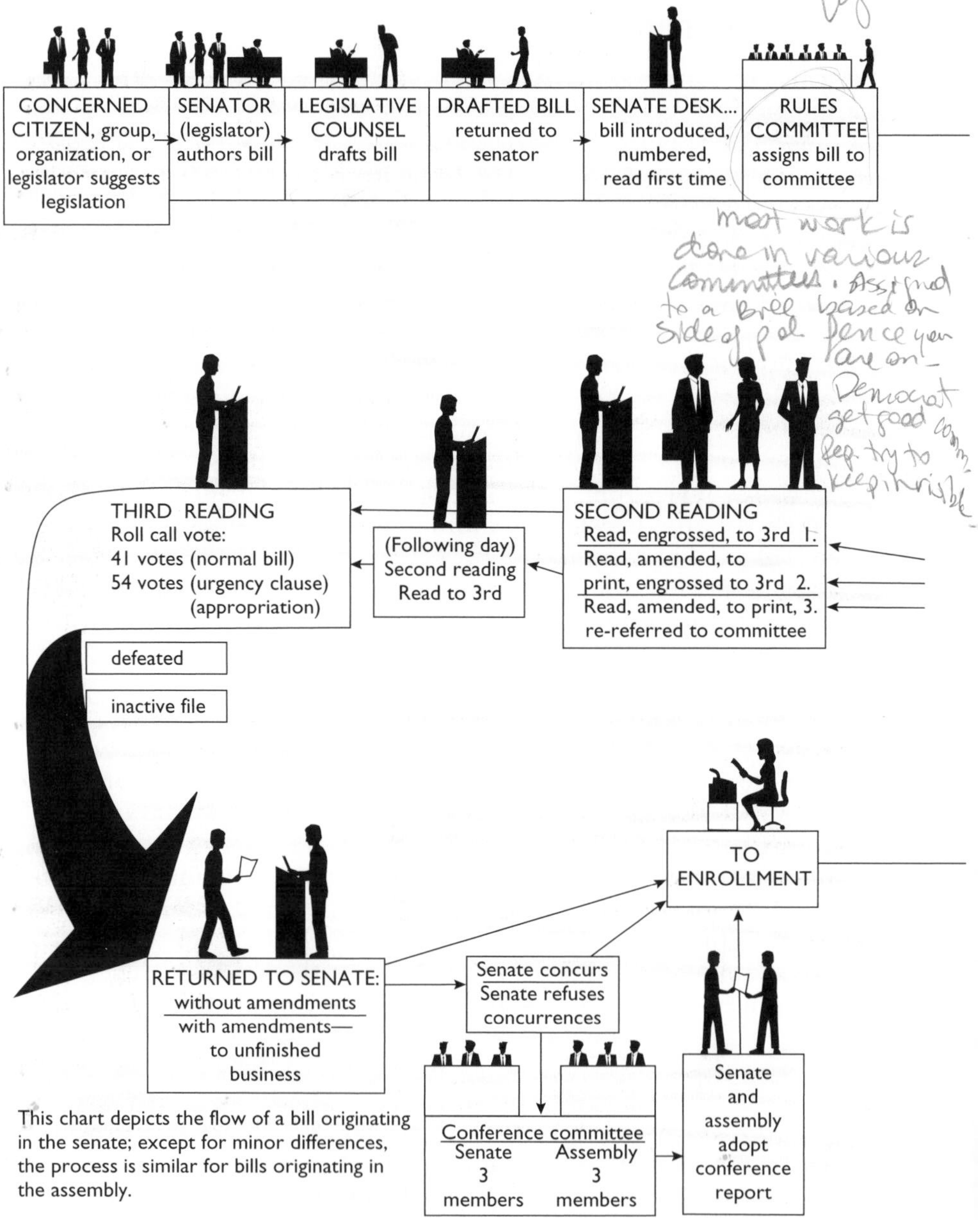

(handwritten margin notes) Democrats in charge of legislature.

(handwritten margin notes) most work is done in various committees. Assigned to a bill based on side of pol. fence you are on. Democrat get good comm. Rep. try to keep invisible.

| CONCERNED CITIZEN, group, organization, or legislator suggests legislation | SENATOR (legislator) authors bill | LEGISLATIVE COUNSEL drafts bill | DRAFTED BILL returned to senator | SENATE DESK... bill introduced, numbered, read first time | RULES COMMITTEE assigns bill to committee |

THIRD READING
Roll call vote:
41 votes (normal bill)
54 votes (urgency clause) (appropriation)

(Following day) Second reading Read to 3rd

SECOND READING
Read, engrossed, to 3rd 1.
Read, amended, to print, engrossed to 3rd 2.
Read, amended, to print, 3. re-referred to committee

defeated

inactive file

RETURNED TO SENATE:
without amendments
with amendments—
to unfinished business

Senate concurs
Senate refuses concurrences

TO ENROLLMENT

Conference committee
Senate Assembly
3 3
members members

Senate and assembly adopt conference report

This chart depicts the flow of a bill originating in the senate; except for minor differences, the process is similar for bills originating in the assembly.

This chart depicts the flow of a bill originating in the senate; except for minor differences, the process is similar for bills originating in the assembly.

SOURCE: California state legislature.

FIGURE 5.2
(CONTINUED)

Most Bills die in committee

BILL PRINTED

COMMITTEE HEARINGS: (No action for 30 days after introduction and printing)

Typical recommendations:
Do pass
Do pass as amended
Amend and re-refer

say what you want to say

Held in committee

too many amendments, no courtesy, send back to original author.

SECOND READING
1. Read, engrossed, to 3rd
2. Read, amended, to print, engrossed to 3rd
3. Read, amended, to print, re-referred to committee

THIRD READING
Roll call vote:
21 votes (normal bill)
27 votes (urgency bill) (appropriation)

defeated

inactive file

COMMITTEE HEARINGS:
Typical recommendations
1. Do pass
2. Do pass as amended
3. Amend and re-refer

Held in committee

SPEAKER OF ASSEMBLY assigns bill to committee

INTRODUCTION and first reading

delivered to **ASSEMBLY DESK**

TO GOVERNOR 12 days to:

sign bill

approve without signature

veto

two-thirds vote in both houses overrides veto

SECRETARY OF STATE (chaptered)

BECOMES LAW on January 1 next following a 90-day period from date of enactment (bills with urgency clause take effect immediately)

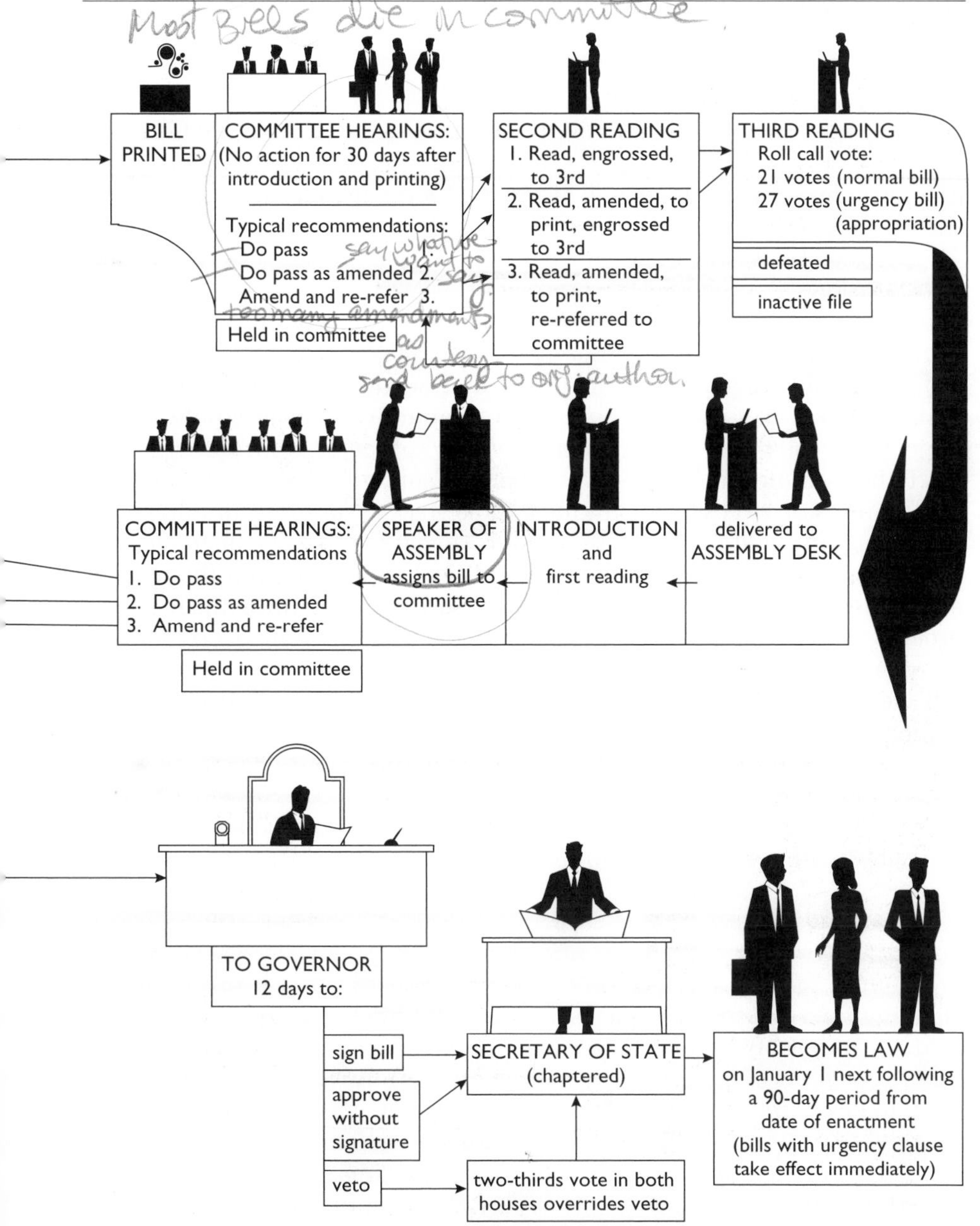

end, the governor has 30 days to act. If the governor vetoes a bill, an absolute two-thirds majority must be attained in both houses for it to become law. Attaining such a lopsided vote is next to impossible, so vetoed bills generally fall by the wayside.

THE INFORMAL PROCESS

Politics penetrates the formal, "textbook" process by which a bill becomes law. This means that every piece of legislation is considered not only on its merits but also on the basis of political support, interest group pressure, public opinion, and personal power.

Partisanship has become more pronounced since the late 1950s, with members of the majority party chairing most, if not all, of the committees in any given year. With Democrats in control for most of the last three decades, they have reaped the benefits of the committee chairs (extra staff, procedural advantages, and so forth) and secured the best committee assignments. Likewise, when assembly Republicans briefly held a bare majority in 1996, they assumed control of 25 of the 26 committees.

Public opinion also affects legislation, sometimes dramatically. Recent statutes on excessive drinking, smoke-free restaurants and bars, assault weapons, and longer sentences for repeat felons have been enacted in direct response to public concern. Political support within the legislature is essential to numerous decisions. So many bills flow through the process that members often vote on measures they haven't even read, relying on staff, committee, or leadership recommendations. Sometimes, a bill's fate may also rest with key legislative leaders, who can use their positions to stifle or speed up a proposal at various points in the legislative process. Outcomes are also affected by **logrolling,** a give-and-take bargaining process in which legislators agree to support each other's bills. More often than not, legislators give away their votes on matters of little concern to them in hopes of mollifying opponents or pleasing powerful leaders.

As noted in Chapter 4, pressure from interest groups permeates the legislative process. With the combined cost of legislative campaigns leaping from $7 million in 1966 to $100 million in 1998, candidates welcomed contributions and, in some cases, accepted them illegally. During this period, the assembly speaker and senate president pro tem became the primary recipients of interest group contributions, directing those dollars, in turn, to key legislative races. The flow of money was astounding; senate President Pro Tem John Burton received nearly $10 million in 1998, easily eclipsing all previous records. Assembly Speaker Antonio Villaraigosa raised $8.2 million during the same year. Proposition 34, enacted in 2002, imposed some constraints on such fund-raising. Thus, in 2002, the cost of state legislative campaigns declined to $76.5 million.[8] Given the innovative efforts of independent campaign committees (unofficial organizations not directly tied to candidates or their campaigns), it remains to be seen whether legislative spending will be contained in the future.

OTHER FACTORS

Finally, personal power within the legislature remains a component of the political process, especially in cases of conflict. One such example occurred in 2000, when senate President Pro Tem John Burton used his power to block Governor Davis's reappointment of the chair of the Board of Prison Terms after the governor appealed a court decision that upheld special care for disabled prisoners.[9] This occurred despite the fact that Davis and Burton both belong to the Democratic party.

Sometimes, the mere threat of an initiative spurs the legislature into action that institutional gridlock might otherwise prevent. In 2003 and 2004, after prodding by both Governors Davis and Schwarzenegger and the early signature-gathering efforts of an initiative proposal, the legislature reformed the state's workers' compensation program.[10] Conversely, the legislature's work on health insurance was undone in November 2004 by a business-sponsored referendum when voters repealed legislation passed in 2003 to require businesses with 50 or more employees to provide health insurance.

UNFINISHED BUSINESS

Today's legislature faces myriad issues, ranging from a questionable public education system to a deteriorating infrastructure. Faced with revolving participants, the legislature operates with little stability and less tradition. Handcuffed by term limits, restrictions on budget growth (see Chapter 8), and recession for most of the last decade, the legislature has struggled to maintain the status quo in most policy areas.

Voter behavior in the 2003 recall election no doubt reflected great frustration with Governor Gray Davis, but the voters also feel plenty of antipathy toward the legislature. Arnold Schwarzenegger tapped into this anger early on in his governorship when he casually suggested one day that perhaps the state would be better off with a part-time legislature.[11] While the voters have blamed the legislature for gridlock, they rejected a ballot measure in 2004 that would have made it easier to pass budgets by reducing the required majority from two-thirds to 55 percent. Other initiatives have proposed "open primaries," such as Proposition 62 in 2004, and reforming legislative redistricting to reduce partisanship in the legislature.

With all these pressures, legislators often seem to react to problems rather than to anticipate or solve them. As a consequence, public policies are made increasingly by initiative, the governor, or the courts. Nevertheless, the legislature continues to grapple with the leading issues of the day, and at least sometimes, lawmakers are able to overcome assorted obstacles and enact policies of substance.

Notes

1. Among the many unusual bills introduced during the 2003–2005 session was one by senate President Pro Tem John Burton, which would have banned the production and sale of foie gras. See "Foie gras flap spreads–bill would ban duck dish," *San Francisco Chronicle,* February 10, 2004, pp. A1, A14.
2. "Schwarzenegger Gets High Job Approval Rating. Voters Expect State Finances To Improve Next Year But Believe Taxes Will Need To Be Raised," *The Field Poll,* Release #2115, May 27, 2004, p. 3.
3. In general, the plan provided one senator per county. In a few cases, two small counties shared a senator, and in one case, three very small counties–Alpine, Inyo, and Mono–shared a senator.
4. Legislators also receive tax-free daily expense stipends; monthly allowances for cars (including gasoline and maintenance); life, health, dental, vision, and disability insurance; and funds to travel between their districts and the capital. On average, these benefits amount to about $30,000 annually.
5. "Plan to Redraw Districts Passes," *Los Angeles Times,* September 14, 2002, p. B8.
6. Kathleen Les, "Mr. Mayor Goes to the Capitol," *California Journal* (Vol. XXX, No. 10, October 1999), pp. 36–38.
7. See "Assembly's Profile Little Changed by Term Limits," *Los Angeles Times,* December 2, 1996, pp. A1, A22.
8. "What Limits? New Law Can't Stop Big Money," *Los Angeles Times,* September 3, 2003, pp. A1, A18.
9. See "Senate Chief Blocks Davis Selection," *Los Angeles Times,* March 10, 2000, pp. A3, A23.
10. "State Fund Posts 9.9% Dip in Comp Rates," *Los Angeles Times,* June 5, 2004, pp. C1, C2.
11. "Gov. Wants a Part-Time Legislature," *Los Angeles Times,* April 7, 2004, pp. A1, A22.

Learn More on the World Wide Web

About the California legislature:

Legislative analyst's office: www.lao.ca.gov

State assembly: www.assembly.ca.gov

State senate: www.senate.ca.gov

About state legislatures:
www.ncsl.org

Learn More at the Library

Bruce E. Cain and Roger G. Noll, Eds., *Constitutional Reform in California*, Berkeley, CA: Institute of Governmental Studies Press, University of California, 1995.

2001–2002 California Political Almanac, 7th edition, California Journal.

Alan Rosenthal, *The Decline of Representative Democracy: Process, Participation and Power in State Legislatures*, Washington, DC: Congressional Quarterly Press, 1998.

See also: The *California Channel* on most cable systems. Watch the legislature at work!

CHAPTER 6

COURTS, JUDGES, AND POLITICS: CALIFORNIA LAW

Courts are very much a part of the political process. Judges and politicians have always known this, but the public has been slower to understand the political nature of the judiciary. When governors made controversial appointments to the courts during the 1970s and 1980s, however, judicial politics became a very public matter. Recently, judicial politics has become apparent in court decisions that have overturned popular initiatives.

What makes the courts political? It's not just controversial judicial decisions or even the involvement of party politicians. Courts are political because their judgments are choices between public policy alternatives. When judges consider cases, they evaluate the issues before them both in terms of existing legislation and in the context of the U.S. and state constitutions. Differing judicial interpretations of these documents help some people and hurt others. This is why the courts, like members of the executive and legislature branches, are subject to the attentions and pressures of California's competing interests, and this is why the courts are political.

THE CALIFORNIA COURT SYSTEM

The California court system–the largest in the nation, with over 2,000 judicial officers–has three levels; each has its own responsibilities, but all are linked. Most cases begin and end at the lowest level. Only a few move up the state's judicial ladder through the appeals process (Figure 6.1). Under certain circumstances, a few state cases may end in the U.S. Supreme Court.

FIGURE 6.1
THE CALIFORNIA COURT SYSTEM

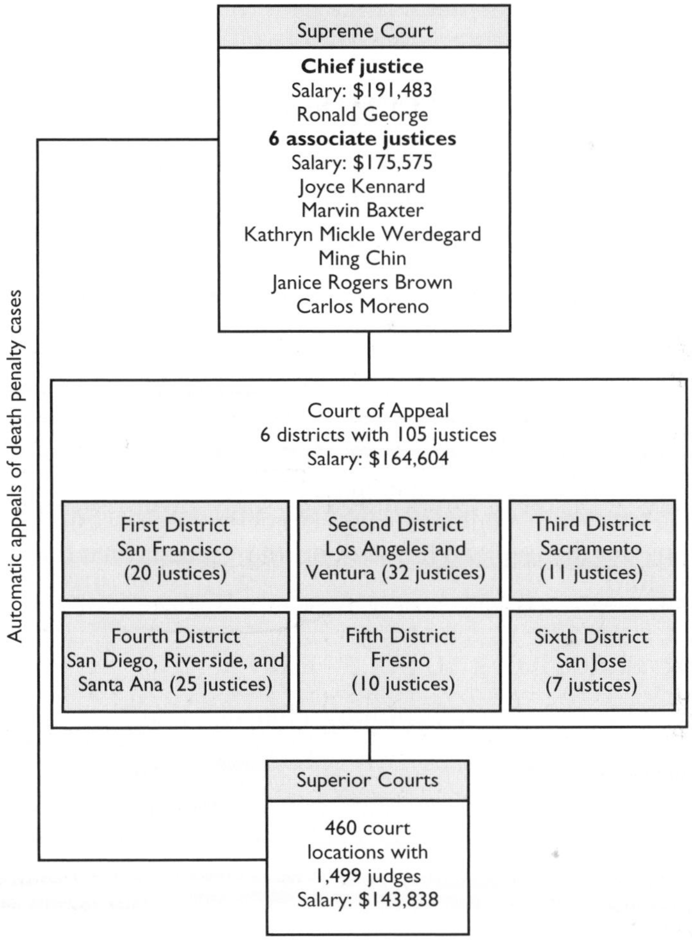

SOURCE: California Judicial Council.

THE JUDICIAL LADDER

The vast majority of cases begin and end in **trial courts,** the bottom rung of the judicial ladder. In California, **superior courts** in each county are the trial courts, handling misdemeanor cases (minor crimes, including most traffic offenses), felonies (serious crimes subject to sentences of 1 year or more in state prison), civil suits (noncriminal disputes), divorces, and juvenile cases. Superior courts also operate small claims courts, where individuals can take cases with damage claims up to $5,000 before a judge without the presence of attorneys–sort of like television's *Judge Judy*.

Losers in trial courts may ask the court on the next rung of the judicial ladder to review the decision. Most cases aren't appealed, but when major crimes and penalties or big money are involved, the losers in the cases sometimes request a review by one of California's six district **courts of appeal.** As appellate bodies, these courts do not hold trials like the ones we see on television. Lawyers make arguments and submit briefs to panels of three justices who try to determine whether the original trial was conducted fairly. If they decide it was not, they can send the case back for another trial or even dismiss the charges.

Ultimately, parties to the cases may petition for review by the seven-member state **supreme court,** the top of California's judicial ladder. Few cases reach this level because most are resolved in the lower courts and the high court declines most petitions. If a case reaches the California Supreme Court, its decision is final unless issues of federal law or the U.S. Constitution arise; the U.S. Supreme Court may consider such cases.

If a higher court refuses an appeal, the lower court's decision stands. Even when a case is accepted, the justices of the higher court have agreed only to consider the issues. They may or may not overturn the decision of the lower court.

JUDICIAL ELECTION AND SELECTION

Although the tiered structure of the California courts is similar to that of the federal courts, the selection of judges is not. Federal judges and members of the U.S. Supreme Court are appointed by the president and confirmed by the U.S. Senate, and they serve for life. California judges and justices, however, gain office through a more complicated process and regularly face the voters. This periodic scrutiny by the public, media, and interest groups helps keep judges and their decisions in the news.

Formal qualifications to become a judge are few: Candidates must have been admitted to practice law in California for at least 10 years. Technically, these judges are elected, but most actually gain office through appointment by the governor when a judge dies, retires, or is promoted between elections. Appointed judges must run for office when the terms of the judges they replace expire, but, running as incumbents, they almost always win. Trial court judges can also gain office simply by declaring their candidacy for a specific judicial office and running. If no candidate wins a majority in the primary election, the two candidates with the most votes face each other in a **runoff election** in November. They serve a 6-year term and then may run for re-election.

APPOINTMENTS AND THE HIGHER COURTS

Unlike lower court judges, members of the district courts of appeal and the state supreme court attain office only through gubernatorial appointment. The governor's possible nominees are first screened by the state's legal community through its Commission on Judicial Nominees Evaluation. Then the nominees must be approved by the **Commission on Judicial Appointments,** consisting of the attorney general, the chief justice of the state supreme court, and the senior presiding judge of the courts of appeal. The commission may reject a nominee, but it has done so only twice since its creation in 1934.

Once approved by the Commission on Judicial Appointments, the new justices take office, but they must go before the voters at the next gubernatorial election. No opponents appear on the ballot; the voters simply check "yes" or "no" on the retention of the justices in question. If approved, they serve the remainder of the 12-year term of the person they have replaced, at which time they can seek voter confirmation for a standard 12-year term and additional terms after that.

A dozen other states select their supreme court justices in a similar fashion, but 26 rely solely on elections. The governor or legislature appoints justices in the remaining 12 states.

FIRING JUDGES

Almost all judges are easily elected and re-elected, mostly without opposition. Those who designed the system probably intended this. They wanted to distance judges somewhat from politics and to ensure their independence by giving them relatively long terms, thus also ensuring relatively consistent interpretation of the law. Avoiding costly election campaigns that depend on financial contributors also promotes independence. The framers of the U.S. Constitution put such a high value on judicial continuity and independence that they provided for selection by appointment rather than by election and allowed judges to serve for life. For most of California's history, these values also seemed well entrenched in its political culture, and the state's judges functioned without much criticism or interference. Nevertheless, the California constitution provides several mechanisms of judicial accountability, all of which have been used recently. Judges can be removed through elections, but they can also be reprimanded or removed by the judicial system itself.

Incumbent justices of the California Supreme Court routinely won re-election without serious challenge until 1966, when a backlash against decisions that supported racial integration led to an unsuccessful campaign to unseat justices who were viewed as too liberal. A few years later, several lower court judges faced challenges because critics viewed them as lenient toward criminals. In 1980, one third of the trial court judges up for election were either defeated or forced into runoff elections.

Although early efforts to oust liberal members of the state supreme court failed, anticourt elements triumphed in 1986, when Chief Justice Rose Bird and two other liberal justices appointed by Governor Jerry Brown were swept out of office. Since then, the anticourt fervor has subsided. Today, sitting judges are rarely challenged.

Judges can also be removed by the judicial system itself. The **Commission on Judicial Performance** was created in 1960 to investigate charges of misconduct or incompetence. Its members include three judges (appointed by the supreme court), two lawyers (appointed by the governor), and six public members (two each appointed by the governor, the senate Rules Committee, and the speaker of the assembly). Few investigations result in any action, but if the charges are confirmed, the commission may impose censure, removal from office, or forced retirement.

Hundreds of complaints against judges are filed with the commission each year; about one third are investigated. In the rare cases in which the commission finds a judge to be at fault, it usually issues a warning. Even more rarely, the commission may remove a judge from the bench. In a recent scandal in San Diego, several judges were admonished for accepting gifts from attorneys who appeared before them. One of their colleagues was removed from office, and two others resigned while under investigation. Two were eventually sentenced to prison. Actual removal from the bench is extremely rare because, like the San Diego judges, those whose conduct is questionable usually resign before the commission's investigation is completed.

THE COURTS AT WORK

In 2002–2003, 7,994,149 cases were filed in California's trial courts. Most of these were criminal cases. About 1.5 million were civil suits on such matters as divorce or contract disputes. Some observers think that this volume of cases is a result of the eagerness of Californians to resolve issues in the courts, spurred on by more than 195,585 attorneys who are members of the California Bar. But a 1995 study found that, on a per capita basis, California's rate of civil disputes is below the national average.[1]

California's constitution guarantees the right to a jury trial for both criminal and civil cases; if both parties agree, however, a judge alone may hear the case. Jurors are drawn from lists of licensed drivers, voters, and property owners, but finding a 12-member jury is often difficult. Many people avoid jury duty because it takes time away from work and pays only a few dollars a day. Homemakers and retired people are most readily available, but they alone cannot make up a balanced jury. Poor people and minorities tend to be underrepresented because they are less likely to be on the lists from which jurors are drawn and because some avoid participation in a system that they distrust.

The parties in civil cases provide their own lawyer, although legal aid societies sometimes help those who can't afford counsel. In criminal cases, the **district attorney,** an elected county official, carries out the prosecution. Defendants hire their own attorney or are provided with a court-appointed attorney if they cannot afford one. California's larger counties have a **public defender** to provide such assistance. Well over half of all felony defendants require court-appointed help.

Most cases never go to trial, however. Nearly 90 percent of all criminal cases are resolved by **plea bargaining,** which results in a pretrial agreement on a plea and a penalty. Plea bargaining reduces the heavy workload of the courts and guarantees some punishment or restitution, but it also allows those charged with a crime to serve shorter sentences than they might have received if convicted of all charges. Most civil suits are also settled without a trial because the parties to the cases often reach an agreement to avoid the high costs and long delays of a trial. Less than 1 percent of all cases are tried before a jury (only 11,517 in 2002–2003); a judge alone hears the rest.[2]

Significantly, the judicial system as a whole–from judges to prosecutors, public defenders, lawyers, and juries–does not reflect the diversity of California's people. Only 17 percent of California's attorneys are nonwhite. A Judicial Council study reports that more than 80 percent of all judges, prosecutors, public defenders, and other court officials are white, while a substantial majority of defendants are not. The study also expressed concern about evidence that punishment is less severe for whites than for minorities convicted of the same crime. African Americans, and to a lesser extent other minorities, perceive this and express deep mistrust of the system.[3]

APPEALS

When a dispute arises over a trial proceeding or its outcome, the losing party may appeal to a higher court to review the case. Most appeals are refused, but the higher courts may agree to hear a case because of previous procedural problems (for instance, if the defendant was not read his or her rights) or because it raises untested legal issues. Appellate courts do not retry the case or review the facts in evidence; their job is to determine whether the trial was fair and the law was applied appropriately. In addition to traditional appellate cases, the state supreme court also automatically reviews all death penalty decisions. Although few in number (27 in 2002–2003), these cases take up a substantial amount of the court's time. A few other cases come to it directly. Known as "original proceedings," these include cases involving writs of mandamus (ordering a government action) and habeas corpus (a request for reasons why someone is in custody). Neither the courts of appeal nor the state supreme court can initiate cases. No matter how eager they are to intervene in an issue, they have to wait for someone else to bring the case to them.

Every year nearly 9,000 petitions are filed with the California Supreme Court, mostly requesting reviews of cases decided by the courts of appeal. Each year the members of the court, meeting "in conference," choose about 200 petitions for consideration, a task that consumes an estimated 40 percent of the court's time. By refusing to hear a case, the court allows the preceding decision to stand. When the court grants a hearing, one of the justices (or a staff member) writes a "calendar" memo analyzing the case. Attorneys representing the two sides present written briefs and then oral arguments, during which they face rigorous questioning by the justices.

After hearing the oral arguments, the justices discuss the case in conference and vote in order of seniority; the chief justice casts the final, and sometimes decisive, vote. If the chief justice agrees with the majority, he or she can assign a justice to write the official court opinion; usually this is the same justice who wrote the initial calendar memo. A draft of the opinion then circulates among the justices, each of whom may concur, suggest changes, or write a dissenting opinion. Finally, after many months, the court's decision is made public. The court issued 123 opinions in 2002–2003–about 1 percent of all the cases filed.

This time-consuming process allows plenty of room for politicking among the justices and depends on a high degree of cooperation and deferential behavior among justices–what judges call **collegiality**–as a way of building consensus on issues before the court. With seven independent minds on the court, ongoing negotiations are needed to reach a majority and a decision.

RUNNING THE COURTS

In addition to deciding cases, the chief justice acts as the administrative head of the California court system. This entails setting procedures for hearings and deliberations, managing public information for the supreme court, and overseeing its staff. The chief justice also assigns cases to specific appellate courts and appoints temporary justices when there are vacancies on the supreme court due to disqualification, illness, or retirement.

As chair of the **Judicial Council,** the chief justice also takes a hand in managing the entire state court system. The Judicial Council has 21 members, including 14 judges (appointed by the chief justice), 4 attorneys (appointed by the state bar association), and 1 member from each house of the state legislature. The Judicial Council makes the rules for court procedures, collects data on the operations and workload of the courts, and gives seminars for judges.

Recent chief justices have exhibited very different styles as managers of the state court system. Chief Justice Rose Bird (1977–1987), a liberal appointed by Governor Jerry Brown, tried to shake up the system and made herself unpopular with the state's legal establishment. The legal profession and the media view Ronald George, the current chief justice, more favorably. Personable and accessible, Chief Justice George has been credited with reinvigorating the courts and their image.

THE HIGH COURT AS A POLITICAL BATTLEGROUND

The courts are particularly important and powerful in California because of the nature of California's government and politics. California's constitution is long and elaborately specific, dealing with all sorts of matters, both major and mundane; its index alone is twice as long as the entire U.S. Constitution. The complexity of California's constitution is reflected in the structures of government it sets out and is increased through constant revision by initiative. In turn, the length, detail, and continually changing complexity of California's constitution give its courts greater power because they have the job of determining whether laws and public policy are consistent with the constitution. One scholar has called the courts a "shadow government"[4] because of their increasing importance in shaping public policy, but others view this as the courts' appropriate constitutional role.

At the top of California's judicial ladder is the state supreme court, the ultimate interpreter of the state constitution (unless issues arise under the U.S. Constitution). The court's power makes it a center of political interest: Governors strive to appoint justices who share their values and pay close attention to the appointment process. A governor who is elected to two terms of office may have appointed as many as half of the state's sitting judges, significantly affecting judicial practices. As governors have changed, so have the sorts of justices they appoint (Table 6.1). And as its membership has changed, the California Supreme Court has moved across the spectrum from liberal to conservative.

Regardless of their collective political values, the court has not backed away from controversial issues, including occasionally overturning decisions by the legislature or the people (as expressed in initiatives). This is less because of interventionist attitudes on the part of the justices than because of a long, complex, and frequently amended constitution and poorly written laws and initiatives.

TABLE 6.1
JUDICIAL APPOINTMENTS BY CALIFORNIA GOVERNORS, 1959–2004

	MALE	FEMALE	WHITE	BLACK	HISPANIC	ASIAN
Edmund G. Brown, Sr.	97.7%	2.3%	93.0%	3.0%	2.5%	1.5%
1959–1967	(390)	(10)	(372)	(12)	(10)	(6)
Ronald Reagan	97.4	2.6	93.1	2.6	3.3	1.0
1967–1975	(478)	(13)	(457)	(13)	(16)	(5)
Jerry Brown	84.0	16.0	75.5	10.9	9.4	4.3
1975–1983	(691)	(132)	(621)	(90)	(77)	(35)
George Deukmejian	84.8	15.2	87.7	3.6	5.0	3.6
1983–1991	(821)	(147)	(849)	(35)	(49)	(35)
Pete Wilson	74.6	25.4	84.4	5.2	4.9	5.5
1991–1998	(517)	(176)	(585)	(36)	(34)	(38)
Gray Davis	65.8	34.2	70.8	9.25	12.8	7.2
1999–2003	(237)	(123)	(255)	(33)	(46)	(26)
Arnold Schwarzenegger	67.0	33.0	100	0	0	0
2003–2004	(2)	(1)	(3)	(0)	(0)	(0)

SOURCE: Governor's Office.

GOVERNORS, VOTERS, AND THE COURTS

Long dominated by liberals, California's supreme court took a distinct turn toward the right in 1986, when the voters rejected Chief Justice Rose Bird and two liberal associate justices. Appointed in 1977 by Governor Jerry Brown, Bird was California's first woman justice. She was a controversial choice because of her liberalism, her lack of experience as a judge, and her age, 40, which was considered young for such a high post.

Once on the court, Bird was criticized for being too sympathetic to criminal defendants, favoring busing as a means of school desegregation, and opposing Proposition 13, the popular property-tax reduction initiative. The voters confirmed Bird's appointment in 1978 by 51.7 percent, the lowest ever in the history of California's judicial elections. Despite her close call, the chief justice and the liberal court majority continued to hand down controversial decisions. Even as public concern about crime increased, for example, they consistently reversed death sentences on what critics viewed as legal technicalities. When the justices were on the ballot in 1986, voters rejected Bird and two other Brown-appointed justices while confirming a less controversial Democrat and two new conservatives appointed by Brown's successor, Republican George Deukmejian.

Soon after, Governor Deukmejian transformed the court with conservative appointees, including a new chief justice.

Subsequent appointees by Republican Governor Pete Wilson maintained the court's conservative majority. Led by Chief Justice Ronald M. George, today's court includes Deukmejian appointees Marvin Baxter and Joyce Kennard and Wilson appointees Kathryn Werdegar, Ming Chin, and Janice Rogers Brown. Carlos Moreno, the court's only Democrat, was appointed by Governor Davis in 2001. Minority members of the court include Moreno (Latino), Brown (African American), Chin (Chinese), and Kennard (Dutch-Indonesian), but as Table 6.1 suggests, women and minorities are underrepresented in the California judiciary as a whole.

The current justices have won voter approval, with 57 to 76 percent voting for their retention. Antiabortion forces targeted Chief Justice George and Justice Chin in their 1998 retention election because of their controversial 1997 votes to reverse a previous court decision that required minors to obtain parental consent for abortions. The worried justices raised $1.6 million for their campaigns, hired consultants, and met with the editorial boards of the state's major newspapers. In the end, both won retention, with 76 percent voting affirmatively for George and 69 percent for Chin.

With a majority of the justices appointed by Republican governors and solidly confirmed by the voters, California's Supreme Court today is moderately conservative and considerably less controversial than in the past. The court's conservatism is reflected in its tendency to be pro-prosecution in criminal cases and pro-business in economic cases. The court also disappointed local governments seeking new taxes with rulings that rigidly applied a requirement for two-thirds voter approval, in accordance with 1978's Proposition 13 (see Chapter 8). Overall, the court avoids judicial activism–making policy through court decisions rather than through the legislative or electoral process.

Courts in other states have demonstrated activism on the issue of equal rights for same sex couples that wish to marry, but when the City and County of San Francisco licensed such marriages in 2004, the California state supreme court ruled the marriages illegal on the basis of state law, as approved by the voters in 2002, rather than ruling on the broader issue of equal rights under the constitution. Similarly, when issues about the timing and procedures for the 2003 recall election came before the court, the justices declined to intervene.

Nevertheless, the court maintains its independence as the third branch of state government, and its impact on state politics remains significant. For example, it has followed the Bird court's precedent of approving state-funded abortions, and in 1995 the "conservative" court surprised some observers with a ruling that banned sex discrimination at a private country club. The court also handed Republican Governor Pete Wilson a defeat in 1997 when it ruled against his plan to privatize the work of the state transportation agency. In another display of independence, the

Republican-dominated court removed a Republican-sponsored initiative on reapportionment from the March 2000 ballot because it included issues other than reapportionment and the state constitution limits initiatives to a single subject. Initiatives have been removed from the ballot only five times before.

More controversially, the courts sometimes overrule decisions of the voters. In 1999, for example, the California Supreme Court struck down a voter-approved initiative statute (or law) allowing gambling on Indian reservations because it conflicted with the state constitution. Proponents put the issue back on the ballot in 2000 as a constitutional amendment, again winning voter approval. The courts have also struck down portions of voter-approved initiatives that require tougher sentences of criminals because they shifted discretion from judges to prosecutors.

Sometimes, the federal courts join the fray. In 1995, for example, a federal judge declared portions of Proposition 187–an initiative that limited public services for immigrants–unconstitutional on grounds that only the federal government has authority over immigration. In 2000, the U.S. Supreme Court rejected California's voter-approved blanket, or "open," primary on the grounds that it violated the rights of free speech and association of political parties. The federal courts have also overturned a series of initiatives on campaign finance, ruling that the contribution limits set by these measures were unconstitutional.

Although these rulings against voter-approved laws appear undemocratic, the state and federal courts were doing their duty by interpreting these controversial propositions not only for their content but also for their consistency with the state and national constitutions. When the courts find an act of another branch of government or of the voters to be contrary to existing law or to the state or federal constitution, it is their responsibility to overturn that law, even if their decision is unpopular. "Periodically, cyclically," said Chief Justice George, "the courts have to exercise their function in a way that brings them into direct collision with the other branches of government and possibly with the public will."[5]

COURTS AND THE POLITICS OF CRIME

Crime has topped the list of voter concerns in California and the nation for most of the last 2 decades. Murder, rape, burglary, gang wars, and random violence seemed all too common. A 1994 Field Poll found that 53 percent of all Californians were either "very" or "somewhat" fearful of being victimized by serious crime, up from 42 percent in 1992.[6] Republicans George Deukmejian and Pete Wilson were elected governor at least partly because they were seen as law-and-order candidates.

Capital punishment was a key issue in the 1980s, when Chief Justice Rose Bird and her liberal colleagues on the supreme court overturned the vast majority of the death penalty cases they reviewed. The voters rejected these liberals in 1986, and since then the supreme court has affirmed most death sentences. The issue has not quite gone away, however. Law-and-order advocates still condemn the lengthy delays in death penalty appeals—up to 10 years for the state courts and another 10 years for the federal courts. Judges who are liberal or merely reluctant may cause some of the delay, but experts estimate that much of it is due to the inability of the courts to find legal counsel for the condemned. Meanwhile, public support for the death penalty has declined from 80 percent in 1992 to 63 percent in 2000. Forensic methods such as DNA testing have revealed wrongful convictions in death penalty cases so frequently that 73 percent of Californians now favor a moratorium on executions.[7]

Along with capital punishment, law-and-order proponents have pushed tougher sentences for other crimes. Beginning in the 1980s, voters passed a series of initiatives that strengthened penalties for many crimes. Then, in 1994, the electorate approved the "three-strikes" initiative. The new law reflected public concern about crime and the view that liberal judges who were "soft on crime" were letting criminals off with light sentences. **"Three strikes"** required anyone convicted of three felonies to serve a sentence of 25 years to life: "three strikes and you're out."

The three-strikes law quickly increased the state's prison population as well as spending on prisons (see Chapter 8). New prisons were built, and operating the state prison system absorbs an ever-growing share of the state budget. With many of the state's worst criminals incarcerated for life, three-strikes prosecutions declined, and so did California's crime rate. Conservatives attribute this to tougher judges and penalties. A University of California study, however, found that "most of the decline in crime had nothing to do with three strikes" because the law applies to such a small percentage of cases.[8] Some experts argue that the declining crime rate is due to economic prosperity and demographics, with fewer people in the age group that is most commonly associated with criminal activity. In any case, crime has resonated far less as an issue in recent statewide elections, including the 2003 recall. Responding to criticism that some criminals were incarcerated for life for relatively minor third-strike crimes such as stealing a pizza or a video, voters considered a softer third-strike provision in a 2004 initiative, but the proposal was defeated after a last-minute campaign led by Governor Schwarzenegger.

Another crime-related issue that was once hot also seems to have cooled off. Governor Davis and the Democrats led the nation in the enactment of gun control laws, but while conservatives and gun-lovers continued to protest, Republican Arnold Schwarzenegger established his credentials as a moderate by accepting these laws.

The debate continues, but as the crime rate declines, so does the political urgency of these issues. In the last few years, education, the economy, and health care have outranked crime as the top concerns of California voters.

POLITICS AND THE COURTS

Crime and other issues discussed in this chapter remind us that the courts play a central role in the politics of our state. Controversies about judicial appointments and decisions make the political nature of the courts apparent, especially when they seem to come into conflict with the will of the electorate as expressed in initiatives, yet the courts are never free of politics. They are in the business of making policy and interpreting the law, and their judgments vary with the values of those who make them.

Notes

1. *San Francisco Chronicle,* March 8, 1995, p. A21.
2. Judicial Council, *2004 Court Statistics Report* (www.courtinfo.ca.gov).
3. Judicial Council Advisory Committee Report on Racial and Ethnic Bias in the Courts, 1997.
4. Charles Price, "Shadow Government," *California Journal,* October 1997, p. 38.
5. *Los Angeles Times,* July 24, 1996.
6. *California Opinion Index,* March 1994.
7. Theodore Hamm, "The Death Penalty," *California Journal,* August 2002, p. 9.
8. Franklin E. Zimring, Sam Kamin, and Gordon Hawkins, *Crime and Punishment in California: The Impact of Three Strikes and You're Out,* Berkeley: Institute of Governmental Studies, 1999, p. 84.

Learn More on the World Wide Web

California's court system: www.courtinfo.ca.gov

State Bar of California: www.calbar.org

California Judges Association: www.calcourts.org

Learn More at the Library

Betty Medsger, *Framed: The New Right Attack on Chief Justice Rose Bird and the Courts,* New York: Pilgrim, 1983.

Preble Stolz, *Judging Judges: The Investigation of Rose Bird and the California Supreme Court,* New York: The Free Press, 1981.

Franklin E. Zimring, Sam Kamin, and Gordon Hawkins, *Crime and Punishment in California: The Impact of Three Strikes and You're Out,* Berkeley, CA: Institute of Governmental Studies, 1999.

CHAPTER 7
THE EXECUTIVE BRANCH: COPING WITH FRAGMENTED AUTHORITY

The **governor** is California's most powerful public official. He or she shapes the state budget, appoints key policy makers in the executive and judicial branches, participates in reapportionment of the legislature and California congressional delegation, and interacts with public opinion by taking positions on controversial issues. There are times when the governor's powers extend even beyond his or her normally broad limits to occasional disasters such as California's massive power crisis in 2001. There are also times when the governor's performance can generate intense reaction from the legislature or public, as evidenced by the historic recall of Governor Gray Davis by the voters in 2003.

Unlike the president of the United States, however, the governor of California shares authority with seven other independently elected executive officers. Occasionally, these other executives clash with the governor over the use of power, as do the legislature and the judiciary. In the past, such fragmentation of executive authority has accounted for occasional standoffs and public pandering. There has been one change in this dynamic, however. Term limits, although applicable to both the executive and legislative branches, have left the governor in a stronger position relative to the legislature because of the near-certainty of two 4-year terms of office.

THE GOVERNOR: FIRST AMONG EQUALS

The current governor, Republican Arnold Schwarzenegger, was elected in 2003 as the result of the removal of Gray Davis from office (Table 7.1). With an annual salary of $175,000, he is the third-highest-paid chief executive of the 50 states, trailing only the governors of New York and Michigan. As California's highest-ranking executive, the governor is the state's chief administrator, the unofficial leader of his political party, and liaison to other states, the U.S. government, and other nations.

TABLE 7.1

California Governors and Their Parties, 1943–2007

Name	Party	Dates in Office
Earl Warren	Republican*	1943–1953
Goodwin J. Knight	Republican	1953–1959
Edmund G. Brown, Sr.	Democrat	1959–1967
Ronald Reagan	Republican	1967–1975
Jerry Brown	Democrat	1975–1983
George Deukmejian	Republican	1983–1991
Pete Wilson	Republican	1991–1999
Gray Davis	Democrat	1999–November 2003
Arnold Schwarzenegger	Republican	2003–

*Warren cross-filed as both a Republican and a Democrat in 1946 and 1950.

Schwarzenegger came to power with little experience in politics. Other than a few minor speaking roles at Republican national conventions, his only serious political involvement in California came in 2002, when he championed Proposition 49, a statewide initiative that dedicated excess budget funds for afterschool programs. Given California's desperate economic plight, the program has not been implemented. Lack of political experience has not interfered with early political success, however. In an election with 135 candidates, Schwarzenegger captured an astounding 49 percent of the vote to easily outdistance his opponents, including Democratic Lieutenant Governor Cruz Bustamante.

Much of the governor's authority comes from formal powers written into the state's constitution and its laws. In addition, certain informal powers derive from the prestige of the office and the ability of a governor to lead public opinion through the "bully pulpit" it provides. Despite his lack of previous political experience, Governor Arnold Schwarzenegger has demonstrated considerable skill in exercising the informal powers of his office.

FORMAL POWERS

No other formal power is more important than the governor's budgetary responsibilities. According to the constitution, the governor must recommend a balanced budget to the legislature within the first 10 days of each calendar year. The governor's proposals usually include requests for both taxing and spending. Budget work is virtually a year-round task for the governor and his or her appointed **director of finance.** The two begin their initial preparations on July 1, the start of the fiscal year, and end with the signing of the budget about a year later.

TABLE 7.2

VETOES AND OVERRIDES, 1967–2004

GOVERNOR	BILLS VETOED	VETOES OVERRIDDEN
Ronald Reagan (1967–1975)	7.3%	1
Jerry Brown (1975–1983)	6.3%	13
George Deukmejian (1983–1991)	15.1%	0
Pete Wilson (1991–1999)	16.6%	0
Gray Davis (1999–November 2003)	17.6%	0
Arnold Schwarzenegger (November 2003–2004)	24.6%	0

The state constitution requires the legislature to respond to the governor's budget no later than June 15 so that the budget can go into effect by July 1, a formidable task because the proposed document is the size of a thick telephone book. Technically, legislators can disregard any or all parts of the budget package and pass their own version, but usually they stay reasonably close to the governor's proposals. They realize that the governor has the final say, albeit with some limitations. The governor cannot add money, but he or she can reduce or eliminate expenditures through use of the item veto before signing the budget into law. An absolute two-thirds vote from each house of the legislature, a near impossibility (see Chapter 5), is necessary to overturn item vetoes. Accordingly, legislators often attempt to head off vetoes by negotiating with the governor in advance.

Whereas the **item veto** is restricted to appropriations measures, the **general veto** allows the governor to reject any other bill passed by the legislature. It, too, can be overturned only by an absolute two-thirds vote in each house. Over a period of more than 20 years, George Deukmejian, Pete Wilson, and Gray Davis exercised general and item vetoes without a single one being overturned by the legislature. Davis used the veto more than any governor in recent memory. During the 2000–2001 legislative year alone, he vetoed a record one fourth of all bills passed by the legislature, less than his 5-year average of 17.6 percent. Arnold Schwarzenegger quickly put the legislature on notice when he vetoed 24.6 percent of the bills that arrived on his desk during the 2003–2004 legislative year. Thus, the veto is a particularly important weapon in the governor's political arsenal (Table 7.2).

Under most circumstances, the governor has 12 days to act after the legislature passes a bill. On the hundreds of bills enacted by the legislature at a session's end, however, the governor has 30 days to act. Only a veto can keep a bill from becoming law. After the governor's time limit has passed, any unsigned or unvetoed bill becomes law the following January (unless the bill is an urgency measure, in which case it takes effect immediately).

If the governor believes that the legislature has not addressed an important issue, he or she can take the dramatic step of calling a special session. On such occasions, the lawmakers must discuss only the specific business proposed by the governor. Sometimes special sessions are called to meet unexpected crises, as in 2003 when, immediately after assuming office, Governor Arnold Schwarzenegger called on the legislature to deal with California's fiscal emergency and expensive workers' compensation program.

On occasion, the governor can make policy by signing an **executive order,** a step that looks similar to legislation. Governors must exercise this power carefully because such moves often lead to lawsuits over the breadth of their powers. Arnold Schwarzenegger quickly signed an executive order to repeal the vehicle license fee, a revenue source that had been restored by Governor Gray Davis to reduce the state deficit but that very much offended many voters.[1] By taking this action, Schwarzenegger honored a crucial campaign promise.

The governor's appointment powers, although substantial, are somewhat more restricted than his or her budgetary authority because others must approve all appointments except personal staff. Moreover, gubernatorial appointees hold only the top policy-making positions in the state system. Before the Progressive reforms, California governors could rely on patronage, or the "spoils" system, to hire friends and political allies. Today, 99 percent of all state employees are not appointed by the governor but rather are selected through a civil service system based on merit. The governor still fills about 2,500 key positions in the executive departments and cabinet agencies, except for the Departments of Justice and Education, whose heads are elected by the public. Together, these appointees direct the state bureaucracy (Figure 7.1).

The state senate must approve most of the governor's appointees. Generally, senate confirmation is routine, but occasionally the governor's choice for a key post is rejected for reasons other than qualifications. On the rare occasions when individuals elected to the executive branch vacate their posts, such as when Insurance Commissioner Chuck Quackenbush resigned in 2000, the governor's nominees must be approved by majorities in both houses of the legislature.

The governor also appoints people to more than 100 state boards and commissions. Membership on some boards, such as the Arts Council and the Commission on Aging, which have only advisory authority, is largely ceremonial. Other boards, however, such as the California Energy Commission (CEC), Public Utilities Commission (PUC), California Coastal Commission (CCC), and California Occupational Health and Safety Administration (Cal-OSHA), make important policies, free from gubernatorial control. Nevertheless, the governor affects key "independent" boards through manipulation of the budget.

Perhaps the most enduring of all gubernatorial appointments are judgeships. The governor fills both vacancies and new judgeships that are periodically created by the legislature. In his 8 years as governor, Pete Wilson filled 693 posts. During his 5 years in office, Gray Davis appointed 360 judges. Arnold Schwarzenegger, however, appointed only 3 in his first year as governor. Most judges continue to serve long after those who appointed them have gone. However, the governor's power is checked here, too, by various judicial commissions and by the voters in future elections (see Chapter 6).

INFORMAL POWERS

Formal constraints on the governor can be offset to some extent by a power that is not written into the constitution at all: the governor's popularity. As the top state official, the governor is highly visible. The attention focused on the office provides a platform from which he or she can influence the public and overcome political opponents.

Historically, California's governors have used the prestige of their office to push their own agendas. Throughout his tenure as governor, Pete Wilson engaged the legislature in protracted budget battles, demanding massive cuts in welfare and virtually all other elements of state spending in exchange for minimal tax increases. Only prisons consistently received Wilson's blessing as recipients of new spending. Almost always, the legislature capitulated after symbolic resistance. More than any of his predecessors, Wilson turned to the public for policy making via ballot propositions. In 1994, he touted **Proposition 187,** an attempt to reduce government benefits to illegal immigrants that was ultimately declared unconstitutional by the federal courts. In 1996, Wilson championed **Proposition 209,** entitled the California Civil Rights Initiative, as a means of eliminating affirmative action. And in 1998, he promoted **Proposition 227,** an initiative restricting bilingual education.

Gray Davis brought his unique brand of politics to the governor's office as well. When the state was suddenly confronted by a severe energy shortage in 2001, he used his executive powers to relax the state's air standards, permitting older, dirtier electricity plants to produce more energy. He also expedited the approval process for new power plants. Davis blamed the state's sudden shortages on the energy producer "robber barons"[2] and demanded the return of more than $9 billion in overcharges by out-of-state power companies to California consumers. By 2002, documents provided by Enron Corporation, an abruptly bankrupt energy company, supported Davis's claim of corporate collusion.[3] Recovering any of the overcharges, however, remained a challenge.

FIGURE 7.1

State Departments and Agencies

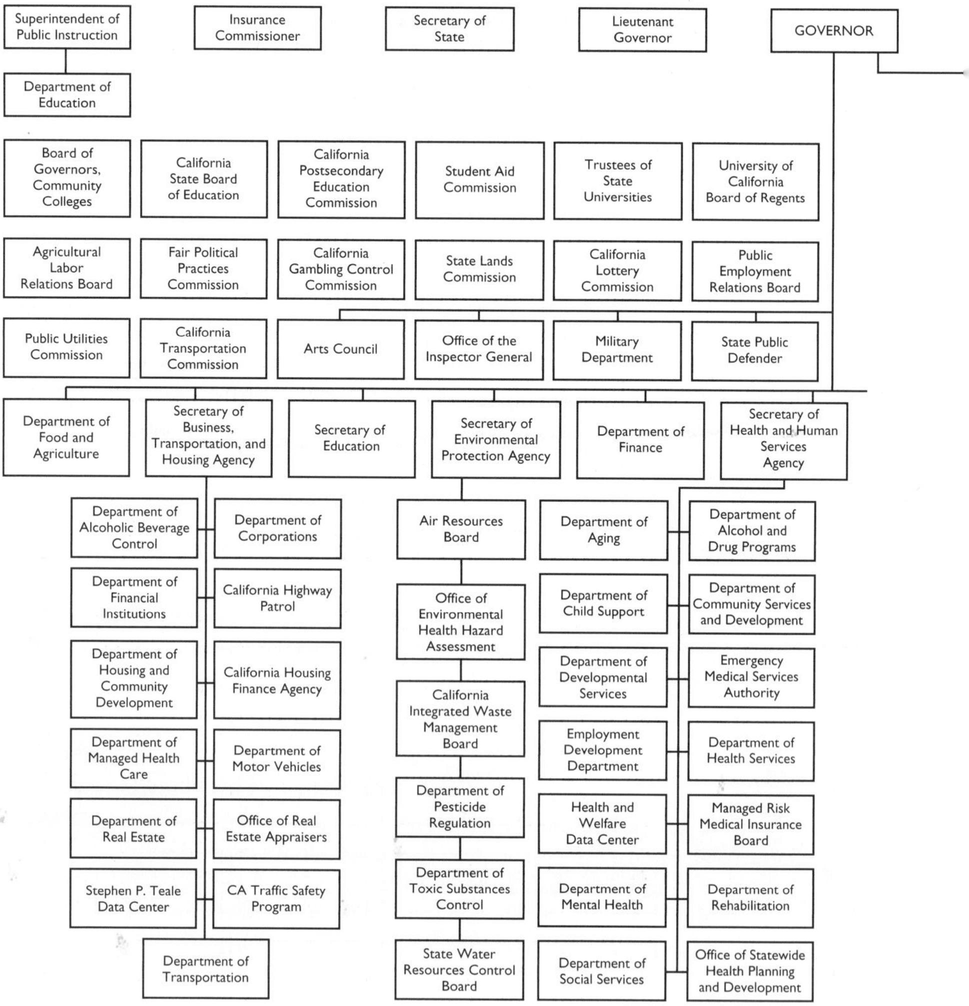

SOURCE: Office of the governor.

FIGURE 7.1
(CONTINUED)

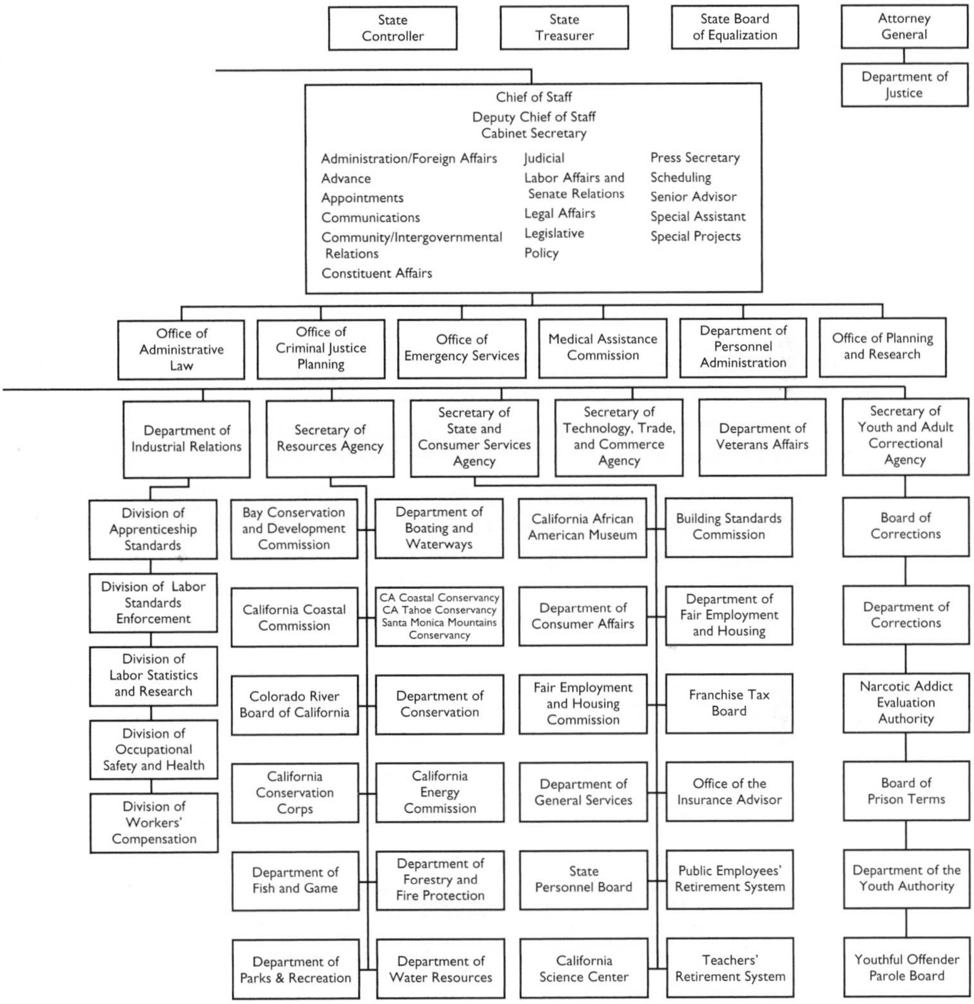

Even though Davis was re-elected after the energy crisis, his problems only worsened. Between the energy crisis, a lengthy recession, and huge budget shortfalls in 2002 and 2003 (see Chapter 8), Davis was confronted with unprecedented challenges. In addition to having his hands full with problems not entirely of his own doing, Davis contributed very directly to his difficulties with the other branches of state government. When discussing legislators in 1999, Davis stated that "their job is to implement my vision."[4] Davis offered similar advice to the state's judiciary in 2000 when he declared that "my [judicial] appointees should reflect my views. They are not here to be independent agents."[5] A seemingly aloof personality and a reputation for constant fundraising from individuals and organizations doing business with the state added to his problems, which ultimately hurt his standing with the public. In a July 2003 Field Poll, 75 percent of the respondents agreed that the state was on the wrong track, and 61 percent put the blame on Davis.[6] Thus, as the recall effort moved along during 2003, Davis lost his reservoir of public support, the ultimate source of a leader's informal power.

Arnold Schwarzenegger, on the other hand, has attempted to utilize his informal powers both by schmoozing and cajoling legislators and by appealing directly to the public. Like Pete Wilson, he's gone directly to the voters with his successful advocacy of Proposition 57 (a $15-billion "recovery" bond) and Proposition 58 (a future reserve fund), both in the March 2004 election. He threatened an initiative on workers' compensation reform as a means to get the legislature to move on the issue. During the 2004 budget negotiations, he went beyond the legislature to cut deals directly with organizations and institutions, from local government to universities, prison guards, and Indian gaming interests. On these and other issues, he's taken his case directly to the public with rallies, usually in shopping centers, which, thanks to his movie-star status, inevitably draw more media coverage than any legislator could ever imagine.

THE SUPPORTING CAST

If California's executive branch were composed solely of the governor, appointed department heads, and the civil service system, it would parallel the federal executive branch. However, the state's executive branch also includes a lieutenant governor, an attorney general, a secretary of state, a controller, a treasurer, an insurance commissioner, a superintendent of public instruction, and a five-member Board of Equalization. All are elected at the same time and serve 4-year terms, but unlike the president and vice president, who are elected on the same political party ticket, each of these officeholders runs independently.

Most other states provide for the election of a lieutenant governor, a secretary of state, a treasurer, and an attorney general, but few elect an education officer, a controller, a Board of Equalization, and an insurance regulator. Moreover, most states call for the governor and the lieutenant governor (and others in some cases) to run as a team, thus providing some executive branch cohesion. Not so in California, where, as a result of independent contests, each elected member of the executive branch is beholden to no one.

The consequences of this system can be quite serious. For example, when Republican Governor Wilson ordered then-Controller Gray Davis, a Democrat, to cut state employee paychecks by 5 percent as part of the state's deficit-reduction package in 1991, Davis refused. Likewise, in 2002, when Governor Davis said that the state would not be able to send welfare checks before the passage of a stalled state budget, fellow Democrat and Controller Kathleen Connell, the individual who actually signed the checks, overruled him. These examples show the extent to which very public fights can occur between two officeholders in the executive branch.

THE LIEUTENANT GOVERNOR

The **lieutenant governor** is basically an executive-in-waiting with few formal responsibilities. If the governor becomes disabled or is out of the state, the lieutenant governor fills in as acting governor. If the governor leaves office, the lieutenant governor takes over. This has happened seven times in the state's history, but the last time was in 1953, when Goodwin Knight replaced Earl Warren, who became Chief Justice of the U.S. Supreme Court. The current lieutenant governor, Democrat Cruz Bustamante, was elected in 1998 and re-elected in 2002. His election is significant for two reasons: First, as a Democrat, Bustamante ended a 20-year pattern of the top two officeholders being from different political parties–at least until Democratic Governor Gray Davis was replaced by Republican Arnold Schwarzenegger in 2003. Second, he is the first Latino to hold statewide office in California since 1872. Still, his future is uncertain because of his role in the recall. Unlike other major Democrats in the state, Bustamante chose to run as candidate to replace Gray Davis with the slogan, "Recall No, Bustamante Yes." His candidacy dismantled any hopes of Democratic "unity" in the recall process. Nor does his presence in the Capitol bode well for unity in the executive branch. The Democratic lieutenant governor has urged the Republican governor to feel free to leave the state to continue his career in movies. "I'll be here keeping an eye on things," Bustamante has said.[7]

The lieutenant governor heads some units, such as the State Lands Commission and the Commission on Economic Development. He or she also serves as president of the state senate, but this job, too, is long on title and short on substance. As senate president, the lieutenant governor may vote to break ties, an event that last occurred in 1976. So minimal are the responsibilities of the lieutenant governor that one recent holder of the job quipped that his biggest daily task was to wake up, check the morning newspaper to see if the governor had died, and then return to bed![8] That description may stretch the point a bit, but not by much, according to many political observers.

THE ATTORNEY GENERAL

Despite the lieutenant governor's higher rank, the **attorney general** is usually considered the second-most powerful member of the executive branch. As head of the Department of Justice, the attorney general oversees law enforcement activities, acts as legal counsel to state agencies, represents the state in important cases, and renders opinions on (interprets) proposed and existing laws. The current attorney general, Democrat Bill Lockyer, was elected to the office for the first time in 1998 and re-elected in 2002. He has used the powers of his office to enforce legislation banning assault weapons, but Lockyer has gained even greater notoriety through his high-profile suits against several energy companies for unjust profits (some partially successful) and against Microsoft for antitrust violations.

Substantial authority and independent election allow the attorney general to chart a course separate from the governor's on important state questions. For example, in 1987 then–Attorney General John Van de Kamp, a Democrat, refused to represent Republican Governor Deukmejian in a lawsuit over Deukmejian's management of a new law, forcing the governor to hire private counsel at the state's expense. Such power gives the attorney general a high public profile, enhancing both the clout and the political standing of the officeholder. Earl Warren, Edmund G. "Pat" Brown, and George Deukmejian all moved up to the governor's office from the position of attorney general.

THE SECRETARY OF STATE

Unlike the U.S. cabinet official who bears the same title, the **secretary of state** of California is basically a records keeper and elections supervisor. The job entails certifying the number and validity of signatures obtained for initiatives, referenda, and recall petitions; producing sample ballots and ballot arguments for the voters; publishing official election results; and keeping the records of the legislature and the executive branch. During his tenure in the office, Republican Bill Jones upgraded the website of the secretary of state's office, increasing accessibility to campaign and lobbying records.

The current secretary of state, Democrat Kevin Shelley, was elected in 2002. A former assembly member from San Francisco, Shelley coauthored Proposition 41 in 2002, a $200-million bond proposition that provided funds for counties to improve voting machines with electronic machines instead of paper ballots. However, Shelley's modernization effort actually brought him bad press when, after some questionable results in several counties, he ordered several local registrars not to use some of the new machines; the registrars sued, revealing a new breach between the state and local governments.[9]

THE SUPERINTENDENT OF PUBLIC INSTRUCTION

The **superintendent of public instruction** heads the Department of Education. He or she is the only elected official in the executive branch chosen by nonpartisan ballot. Candidates are identified only by their name and vocation on the primary ballot. Unless one wins a majority, the top two candidates face each other in the November general election. The current superintendent of public instruction, former Democratic state senator Jack O'Connell, was elected in 2002. While in the legislature, he authored Proposition 39 in 2000, which, after passage by the voters, reduced the requirements for approval of local school bonds from two thirds to 55 percent.

In general, the electorate knows little about the candidates for superintendent of public instruction, but teachers' unions, education administrators, and other affected groups take great interest in the choice of superintendent because this official oversees California's massive public education system. The superintendent's powers are severely limited, however, because funding is determined largely by the governor's budgetary decisions, and policies are closely watched by the governor-appointed state board of education and the education committees of the legislature. In 2004, Governor Schwarzenegger proposed a major reorganization of the fractured administrative system, concentrating education policy making in his own office, but the legislature and the education establishment firmly opposed such a reform.

THE MONEY OFFICERS

Perhaps the most fractured part of the executive branch is the group of elected officials who manage the state's money. Courtesy of the Progressive reformers who feared a concentration of power, the controller, the treasurer, and the Board of Equalization have separate but overlapping responsibilities in this area. The **controller** supervises all state and local tax collection and writes checks for the state, including those to state employees. The controller is also an *ex officio* (automatically, by virtue of the office) member of several agencies, including the Board of Equalization, the Franchise Tax Board, and the State Lands Commission. Of all the "money officers," the controller is the most powerful and thus the most prominent. The current controller, Democrat and former high-tech executive Steve Westly, was elected in 2002 in his first run for statewide office. Unlike many leading Democrats in the state, he joined Governor Arnold Schwarzenegger in campaigning for passage of Proposition 57, the $15-billion bond to balance California's books in 2003–2004.

Between taxing and spending, the **treasurer** invests state funds until they are needed for expenditures. Phil Angelides, former state Democratic party chair, was elected to this office in 1998 and re-elected in 2002. For years, the treasurer's position remained almost hidden from public view because of inactivity. But with the growing importance of short-term investments, especially during lean budget years, the office has become better known. In 2002, Angelides used the powers of his office to refinance California's long-term debt, saving the state $1 billion.[10] Unlike Steve Westly, Angelides criticized Proposition 57 as an irresponsible way of handling California's fiscal crisis.

The **Board of Equalization** is also part of California's fiscal system. A product of reform efforts to ensure fair taxation, it oversees the collection of excise taxes on sales, gasoline, and liquor. The board also reviews county assessment practices to ensure uniform calculation methods and practices. The board has five members–four who are elected in districts of equal population and the controller, who serves as chair. Because its tasks lie in the backwaters of state politics, the board's incumbents usually return again and again. Many critics say that the board is an unnecessary vestige of the past; nevertheless, all efforts to eliminate it have proved unsuccessful.

THE INSURANCE COMMISSIONER

The office of **insurance commissioner** exemplifies the persistent reform mentality of California voters. Until 1988, the office was part of the state's Business, Housing, and Transportation Agency, but soaring automobile insurance rates led to Proposition 103, a 1988 initiative that called for 20-percent across-the-board reductions in insurance premiums and made the position of insurance commissioner elective. The scandal surrounding the tenure of Insurance Commissioner Chuck Quackenbush (1994–2000) once again raised the question of whether this office should be elective.

The first elected insurance commissioner, Democrat John Garamendi (1990–1994), obtained about $700 million of the possible $2.5 billion in rebates resulting from Proposition 103. In 1994, Garamendi's successor, Republican Chuck Quackenbush, pursued a policy of insurance industry self-regulation rather than rebates. His approach drew considerable criticism after the massive 1994 Northridge earthquake. Public records showed that several insurance companies had intentionally mishandled claims, leading department staff to recommend hundreds of millions of dollars in fines. Instead, Quackenbush allowed token contributions to his favorite charities and foundations as payment.[11] This arrangement provoked an investigation by the legislature, leading to Quackenbush's resignation in July 2000.

John Garamendi was once again elected insurance commissioner in 2002. Attempting to show independence, Garamendi campaigned for the post without taking any money from insurance interests. During his second tour of duty, Garamendi has been outspoken on workers' compensation reform and consolidation of the health insurance industry.

THE BUREAUCRACY

Elected officials are just the most observable part of the state's administrative machinery. Backing them up, implementing their programs, and dealing with citizens on a daily basis are about 300,000 state workers–the bureaucracy. Only about 5,000 of these workers are appointed by the governor or by other executive officers. Of the rest, 90,000 work at the University of California and California State University. The remainder are hired and fired through the state's civil service system on the basis of their examination results, performance, and job qualifications. The Progressives designed this system to insulate government workers from political influences and to make them more professional than those who might be hired out of friendship.

The task of the bureaucracy is to carry out the programs established by the policy-making institutions–the executive branch, the legislature, and the judiciary, along with a handful of regulatory agencies. However, because bureaucrats are permanent, full-time professionals, they sometimes influence the content of programs and policies, chiefly by advising public officials or by exercising the discretion built into the laws that define bureaucratic tasks. The bureaucracy can also influence policy through the lobbying efforts of its employee organizations (see Chapter 4).

State bureaucrats work for various departments and agencies (Figure 7.1), each run by an administrator who is appointed by the governor and confirmed by the senate. Although civil servants are permanent employees, most administrators serve at the governor's pleasure and must resign at his or her demand. Sometimes political appointees and civil servants clash over the best ways to carry out state policy. If the bureaucracy becomes too independent, the governor can always use his or her budgetary powers to bring it back into line.

Some observers have criticized California's bureaucracy as unnecessarily inflated and unresponsive, even though the size of the state's system ranks 48th on a per capita basis.[12] Thus, Arnold Schwarzenegger promised to "blow up the boxes" on the state's organizational chart, blaming bureaucracy in part for the budget crisis. Shortly after taking office, he appointed a 275-member task force to challenge the status quo. The group responded in 2004 with a 2500-page report that recommended significant reorganization of the state bureaucracy.[13] While some of their suggestions will surely come to fruition, most will meet resistance from the bureaucratic agencies they would affect as well as their allies in the legislature and interest groups they serve.

MAKING THE PIECES FIT

The executive branch is a hodgepodge of independently elected authorities who serve in overlapping and conflicting institutional positions. Nobody, not even the governor, is really in charge. Each official simply attempts to carry out his or her mission with the hope that passable policy will result. Occasionally, reformers have suggested streamlining the system by consolidating functions and reducing the number of elective offices, but the only recent change has been the addition of yet another office, that of insurance commissioner.

Despite these obstacles, the officeholders–most notably governors–have been able to effect some change. George Deukmejian appointed conservative judges, toughened law enforcement, promoted new prisons, and loosened a multitude of regulations on business. Pete Wilson waged war against illegal immigrants, affirmative action, and bloated welfare while continuing to trumpet the "law-and-order" theme. Gray Davis was instrumental in responding to the state's power shortage crisis. Arnold Schwarzenegger challenged the organization of California's bureaucracy.

But the governor does not operate alone. He or she must contend with other members of the executive branch, a suspicious legislature, independent courts, a professional bureaucracy, and most of all, an electorate with a highly erratic collective pulse. Whether these conditions are challenges or impediments, they make the executive branch an interesting part of California government.

Notes

1. "Schwarzenegger Sworn In, Rescinds Car Tax Increase," *Los Angeles Times,* November 18, 2003, pp. A1, A18.
2. "Davis Takes on 'Robber Barons,'" *San Francisco Chronicle,* June 17, 2001, p. A16.
3. "Californians Call Enron Documents The Smoking Gun," *The New York Times,* May 8, 2002, pp. 1A, C6.

4. "Tensions Flare Between Davis and His Democrats," *Los Angeles Times,* July 22, 1999, pp. A1, A28.
5. "Davis Comments Draw Fire," *San Jose Mercury News,* March 1, 2000, p. 14A.
6. The Field Poll, Release #2074, July 15, 2003.
7. "Hijinks: While the Cat's Away," *California Journal,* November 2003, p. 7.
8. "The Most Invisible Job in Sacramento," *Los Angeles Times,* May 10, 1998, pp. A1, A20.
9. See "E-Voting: 1 County Sues State," *Los Angeles Times,* May 5, 2004, pp. B1, B8; and "He Pushed the Hot Button of Touch-Screen Voting," *The New York Times,* June 15, 2004, p. A14.
10. "Angelides: Refinance to Trim Deficit," *Los Angeles Times,* January 4, 2002, pp. B1, B10.
11. See "Quackenbush Rejected Steep Fines for Insurers," *Los Angeles Times,* April 2, 2000, pp. A1, A26.
12. "State Government Employees," Governing, 2004 State and Local Source Book, p. 44.
13. For some of the highlights, see "California Performance Review: Breaking Down the Governor's Proposals," *San Francisco Chronicle,* August 4, 2004, p. A14.

Learn More on the World Wide Web

Daily news summaries: www.rtumble.com
Office of the attorney general: www.caag.state.ca.us
Office of the governor: www.governor.ca.gov
Office of the lieutenant governor: www.ltg.ca.gov
Office of the secretary of state: www.ss.ca.gov
Office of the state board of equalization: www.boe.ca.gov
Office of the state controller: www.sco.ca.gov
Office of the state insurance commissioner: www.insurance.ca.gov
Office of the state treasurer: www.treasurer.ca.gov
Office of the superintendent of public instruction: www.cde.ca.gov/eo

Learn More at the Library

Gary G. Hamilton and Nicole Woolsey Biggart, *Governor Reagan, Governor Brown: A Sociology of Executive Power,* New York: Columbia University Press, 1984.

Gerald C. Lubenow, Ed., *California Votes: The 2002 Governor's Race and the Recall,* Berkeley, CA: Institute of Governmental Studies, University of California, 2004.

Chapter 8
TAXING AND SPENDING: BUDGETARY POLITICS AND POLICIES

No issue is more critical to Californians than taxation, and no resource is more important to state policy makers than the revenues generated from taxation. Yet even though most people may agree on the need for taxes in principle, they often disagree on how much should be collected and how the money should be spent. When policy makers seem to stray from general public values on budgetary issues, the voters are not shy about using direct democracy to reorder the state's fiscal priorities–and with the annual state budget exceeding $100 billion, much is at stake.

Unlike the national government, which usually operates with a deficit, states are supposed to spend only as much money as they collect. This has been difficult in California, where a steady flow of immigrants, a burgeoning school-age population, massive attention to crime, and reduced federal defense spending have challenged a state budget process known more for its limits than for its vision. California fell on particularly hard times in 2002. After several years of revenue surpluses, the state suffered from recession. By 2003, the projected revenue deficit was not only the largest gap in state history, but more than the deficits of the other 49 states combined. Unprecedented political turmoil resulted, with Democratic Governor Gray Davis paying the ultimate price with his historic recall from office later in the year.

All of this was supposed to change with the fresh approach of Arnold Schwarzenegger. Although he promised a balanced budget, the completed document contained many of the frailties found in the preceding one completed under Gray Davis. By relying on hoped-for revenues from the federal government, deferred expenditures, and projects from income sources not even considered by the legislature, Schwarzenegger provided his version of a "balanced" budget. In fact, the budget was $8 billion out of balance immediately upon signature, according to Elizabeth Hill, the state legislative analyst,[1] leading most seasoned observers to believe Schwarzenegger's promise of "no new taxes" would be broken sooner rather than later. The 2004–2005 budget was not signed until July 31, making it the third straight year in which the budget was at least a month late.

THE BUDGETARY PROCESS

Budget making is a complicated and lengthy activity in California. Participants include the governor and various executive-branch departments, the legislature and its support agencies, the public (via initiative and referendum), and occasionally the courts, when judges uphold or overturn commitments made by the other policy makers.

THE GOVERNOR AND OTHER EXECUTIVE OFFICERS

Preparation of the annual budget is the governor's most important formal power. Other policy makers participate in the budgetary process, but none has as much clout because the governor both frames the document before it goes to the legislature and refines it after it leaves the legislature through use of the item veto on budget items that he or she opposes.

During the preceding summer and fall, the governor's director of finance works closely with the budget heads of each state department. Supported by a staff of fiscal experts, the director of finance gathers and assesses information about the anticipated needs of each department and submits a "first draft" budget to the governor in late fall. The governor presents a refined version of this draft to the legislature the following January. The state constitution gives the legislature until June 15 to respond. The annual budget is supposed to take effect on July 1, although it has been late for 15 of the last 20 years.

LEGISLATIVE PARTICIPANTS

Legislative agreement on the budget is often difficult to achieve because, as a "money" bill, it requires an absolute two-thirds vote of approval in each house. Often completed well after the deadline, the budget is a blueprint for the state's annual policy commitments. In a sense, the final vote is anticlimactic because many crucial budgetary decisions are made earlier in the year.

On receiving the budget in January, the legislature's leaders do little more than refer the document to the legislative analyst. Over the next 2 months, the legislative analyst and his or her staff scrutinize each part of the budget with respect to needs, costs, and other factors. Often, the analyst's findings clash with those of the governor, providing the legislature with an independent source of data and evaluation.

Meanwhile, two key legislative units–the assembly's Ways and Means Committee and the senate's Budget and Fiscal Review Committee–guide the budget proposal through the legislative process. After these committees' staffs spend about 2 months going through the entire document, each house assigns portions to various other committees and their staffs. During this time, lobbyists, individual citizens, government officials, and other legislators testify on the proposed budget before committees and subcommittees.

By mid-April, the committees conclude their hearings, combine their portions into a single document, and bring the budget bill to their respective full house for a vote. Should the houses differ on specifics, the bill goes to a two-house conference committee for reconciliation, after which both houses vote again. As June nears and the two houses hone their versions, key legislative leaders and the governor enter into informal negotiations over the document that the legislature and governor will ultimately approve. Known as the **Big Five,** the governor, the speaker of the assembly, the president pro tem of the senate, and the minority party leaders of each house become the nucleus of the final budgetary debate.

THE PUBLIC

Historically, the public has used initiatives or referenda to shape the budget. The voters have relied on ballot propositions to approve the sales tax (1933) and repeal the inheritance tax (1982). Perhaps the most dramatic tax-altering event came in 1978 with the passage of **Proposition 13,** an initiative that reduced local property taxes by 57 percent. Over the next 20 years, property owners saved more than $195 billion in taxes,[2] while local governments became increasingly dependent on the state for relief. As a result, the state has become the major funding agent for local services such as public education, although support has varied with the health of the economy. This uncertainty has brought endless criticism from local government officials.

The voters addressed the tax issue again in 1993. After Governor Wilson redirected $2.4 billion in state funds from local governments to reduce the state's deficit, he and the legislature received voter approval of **Proposition 172,** a measure that increased the state sales tax by 0.5 percent and earmarked new revenues exclusively for public safety provided by local governments. Yet, when the Governor Schwarzenegger attempted to deal with an unbalanced budget in 2004, one of his first acts was to delete $1.3 billion in state funds from local governments, in exchange for more state money down the road. In November 2004, the voters passed **Proposition 1A,** an initiative designed to prevent the state from taking vehicle license fees, sales taxes, and property taxes from local governments in times of economic uncertainty.

THE COURTS

Questions about the legality of various state taxes and programs sometimes make the courts major players in the budgetary process. Judicial involvement is necessary occasionally because of "quick fixes" to complex budget issues that are enacted by public policy makers or the voters.

In 1994, state courts rejected Governor Wilson's plan to pay state workers with IOUs (officially known as *scrip*) while he and the legislature fought over a deficit-riddled state budget. State Controller Kathleen Connell suffered a similar fate in 1998 when a superior court judge blocked her from paying state workers and an array of state bills without a state budget in place. Even the will of the voters has been subject to judicial review, particularly in the many cases arising from the tax-limitation rules and procedures of Proposition 13.

REVENUE SOURCES

Like most states, California relies on several forms of taxation to fund its budget. The largest sources of revenue are personal income tax, sales tax, and bank and corporation taxes. Smaller revenue supplies come from motor vehicle, fuel, insurance, tobacco, and alcohol taxes. The state's major revenue sources and expenditures for fiscal year 2004–2005 are shown in Figure 8.1.

Other taxes are levied by local governments. Chief among these is the property tax, although its use was reduced considerably by Proposition 13. This tax is not collected by the state, but it still is a part, directly or indirectly, of the tax burden of all Californians.

All too aware of the state's antitax mood, policy makers have refused to add taxes to cope with burgeoning needs. As a result, the state's commitments to most services have decreased considerably in recent years. Individual recipients, school districts, and local governments have been thrown into turmoil; infrastructure work such as repairs after the 1989 and 1994 earthquakes and highway maintenance programs have been stretched out. In fact, California now ranks 48th of the 50 states in per capita highway expenditures.

THE SALES TAX

Until the Great Depression of 1929, the relatively small state government relied on minor taxes on businesses and utilities for funds. After the economic crash, however, the state was forced to develop new tax sources to cope with hard times. The first of these, a 2.5 percent **sales tax,** was adopted to provide permanent funding for schools and local governments.

FIGURE 8.1

CALIFORNIA'S REVENUE SOURCES AND EXPENDITURES, 2004–2005

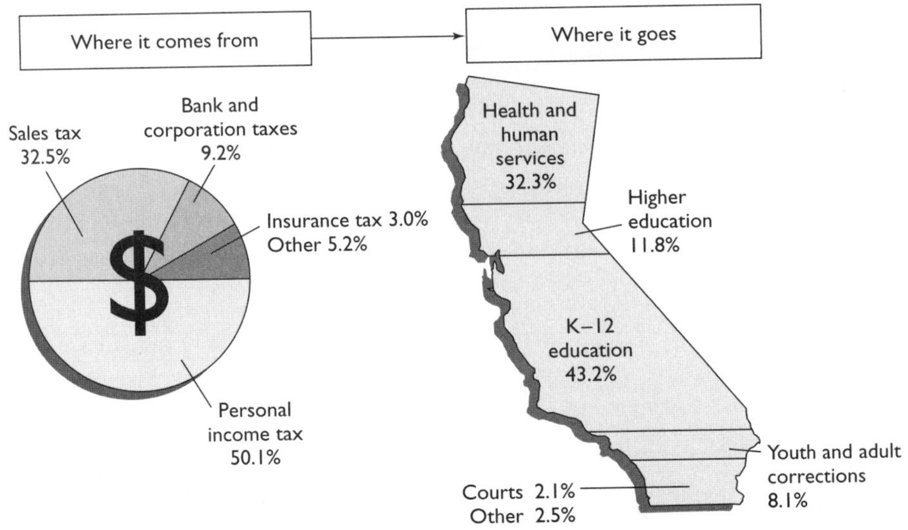

SOURCE: Governor's office.

Today, the statewide sales tax is 7.25 percent; as much as 1.25 percent is tacked on by counties engaged in state-approved projects, most of which are transportation related. Of the basic 7.25 percent, cities and counties get 2 percent, some of which is allocated to transportation and public safety. The state keeps the rest.

Occasionally, the legislature temporarily adjusts the sales tax in response to economic conditions. The last such adjustment occurred in 1989, when a major earthquake in Northern California prompted the legislature and governor to tack on an additional 0.25 percent for 13 months to pay for major road repairs. In 1991, Republican Governor Pete Wilson and the legislature cut the sales tax by 0.25 percent when the state enjoyed a budget surplus of 4 percent or more for 2 successive years. This reduction remained in place until 2002, when the revenue shortfall forced an adjustment upward. In response to the budget crisis in 2004, Governor Schwarzenegger persuaded voters to approve Proposition 57, which provided $15 billion in bonds, or borrowed money, to be repaid over the next decade by diverting 0.25 percent of local governments' share of the sales tax. Today, the sales tax accounts for about 32.5 percent of the state's tax revenues.

FIGURE 8.2
CALIFORNIA'S TAX BURDEN, 1942–2004

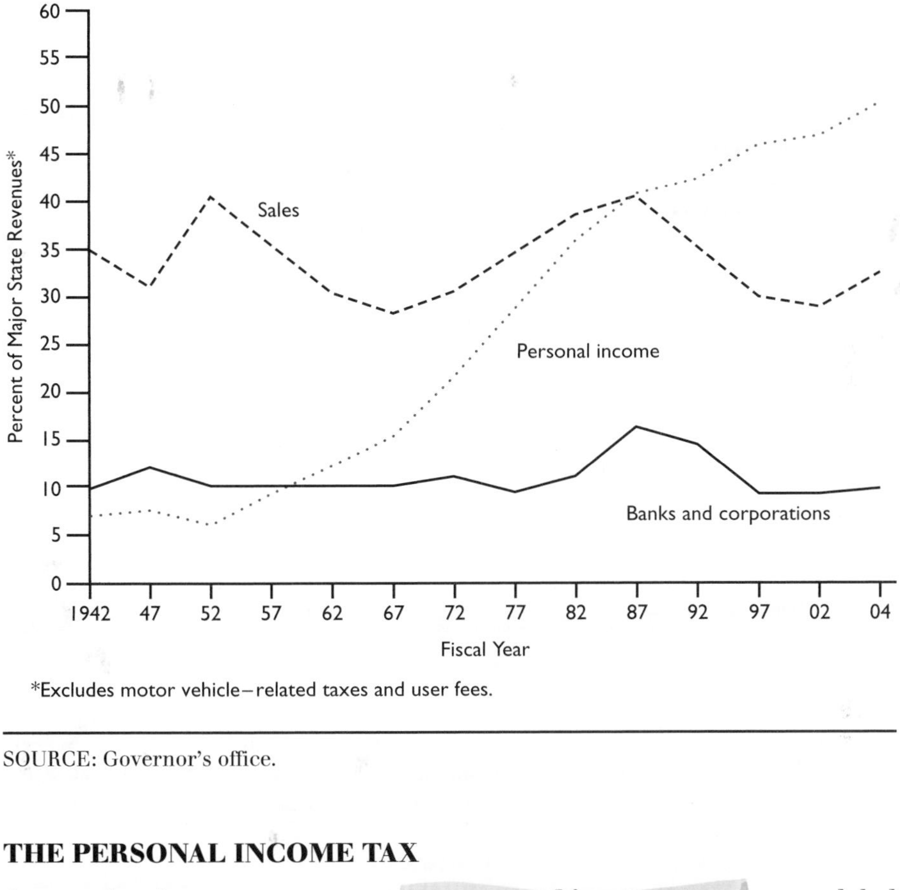

*Excludes motor vehicle–related taxes and user fees.

SOURCE: Governor's office.

THE PERSONAL INCOME TAX

A second major revenue source, the **personal income tax,** was modeled after its federal counterpart to collect greater amounts of money from those residents with greater earnings. Today the personal income tax varies between 1 and 9.3 percent, depending on one's income. State lawmakers and Governor Wilson increased the tax on the highest incomes to 11 percent in 1991, but Wilson argued for and won a reduction to 9.3 percent beginning in January 1996.

The personal income tax is now the fastest-growing component of state revenue (Figure 8.2), a significant fact because Californians ranked ninth in per capita income in 2003. In as much as the tax goes up with increasing incomes, it filled the state coffers with the dramatic economic recovery through most of the 1990s. As of 2004, the tax accounted for 50.1 percent of the state tax bite.

BANK AND CORPORATION TAXES

Financial industry and corporation taxes contribute much less than sales and personal income taxes. Taxes on banks and corporations did not exceed 5.5 percent until 1959, when the legislature enacted a series of rate increases. The last increase occurred in 1980, when, responding to local governments' losses from Proposition 13, the legislature boosted the **bank and corporation tax** from 9.6 percent to 11.6 percent. Between 1987 and 1996, however, the legislature reduced the tax to 8.8 percent, where it remains for corporations today. Since 1996, the corporate tax for banks has been fixed at 10.8 percent. Together, bank and corporation taxes now account for about 9 percent of state revenues.

Aside from Proposition 13 and the expanded reliance on **user taxes,** such as those levied on gasoline and cigarettes, California's revenue collection system has undergone gradual adjustments over the past 60 years. Shown in Figure 8.2 are the changing influences of the sales, personal income, and bank and corporation taxes from 1942 to the present. Recent data indicate a steady drift toward increased dependence on the personal income tax and decreased dependence on the sales tax.

OTHER SOURCES

From time to time, state leaders have asked voters to approve bonds, thus obligating the electorate to long-term commitments. These projects, sometimes lasting as long as 40 years, finance major infrastructure commitments such as school classrooms, highways, and water projects. The state has turned to bonds with increasing frequency. In 1991, California ranked 32nd among the 50 states in indebtedness on a per capita basis; by 2004, the state had climbed to 10th place, with an indebtedness of about $41 billion. The state's per capita indebtedness of $1,170 is now about 10 percent above the national average, including the $15 billion "recovery" bond passed by the voters as Proposition 57 in 2004. Because of its increasing debt, California now has one of the lowest credit ratings of any state, which increases the interest costs that the state must pay to retire the bonds.

California also gets a small but growing portion of its revenue from fees and charges for services. For example, 90 percent of the operating costs of state parks were funded by taxes in 1982–1983, but within a decade, only 40 percent came from tax revenues, while 57 percent came from fees and concessions. Although Governor Davis and the legislature reduced those fees in 2000, new budget pressures led Governor Schwarzenegger and the legislature to increase them again in 2004.

TAXES IN PERSPECTIVE

Viewed in a comparative context, the overall tax burden for California ranks 10th in the nation on a per capita basis, remarkably close to its per capita income ranking. Nevertheless, there have been changes in the state tax blend, with the state becoming increasingly dependent on the personal income tax as its primary source of income.

When calculating state and local taxes as a percentage of personal income, California ranks 19th. On a per capita basis, the state ranks 19th in sales taxes, 7th in personal income taxes, 9th in bank and corporation taxes, and 33rd in property taxes.

In other areas, California taxes are near the bottom, due largely to the influence of powerful interest groups. For example, the state ranks 49th in both fuel taxes and alcoholic beverage taxes. Cigarette taxes stand out as a prominent exception due to a voter-approved initiative in 1998, which moved the state into 3rd place behind Minnesota and Hawaii; however, by 2003, the state fell to 19th.

Balancing budget revenues and expenditures has not always been easy for state leaders. Between 1991 and 1995, the state budgetary process was hobbled by an unrelenting recession and its by-product, inadequate revenues. Annual budget shortfalls of between $5 billion and $14 billion ensued, often forcing Governor Wilson and the recession-weary legislature to raise taxes and borrow billions from banks just to make ends meet. Beginning in 1996, the state recovered, leading to the huge surpluses of 1999–2001. As a result, Governor Davis and the legislature agreed on increased spending and a modest tax refund. The state economy soured considerably in 2002, leaving a huge revenue gap that approached $38 billion by early 2003. With Governor Davis and the legislature unable to reach agreement on a response to the crisis, the state's budget-making process tumbled out of control. No doubt, this problem contributed to the removal of Davis by the voters in the October 2003 recall election.

SPENDING

The annual state budget addresses thousands of financial commitments, both large and small. Major areas of expenditure include public education (grades K through 12), health and welfare, higher education, and prisons. Outlays in these four areas account for more than 80 percent of the general fund. The remainder of the budget (the difference between total expenditures and the general fund) goes to designated long-term projects such as transportation, parks, and veterans' programs, many of which have been authorized by public ballot.

Since 1979, state spending has been determined more by the public than by the legislature and the governor. Under Proposition 4 (1979) and Proposition 111 (1990), budgets have been determined largely by formulas rather than by need. In 2004–again at the urging of Governor Schwarzenegger–the voters passed **Proposition 58,** which requires the state to gradually set aside up to 3 percent of all revenues in a "rainy day" fund, beginning in 2006. Critics have characterized the formula approach as a political "straitjacket" that is unresponsive to changing times and needs, particularly in light of decreasing federal support and a shrinking defense industry in California. Defenders of "formula government" argue that it is the only way to keep state leaders from operating with a "blank check."

PUBLIC EDUCATION: GRADES K THROUGH 12

With the state constitution giving public education a "superior right" to state funds, public schools get the largest share of state expenditures. Public education funding became largely a state government obligation in 1972 when, in ***Serrano v. Priest,*** the state supreme court held that local property tax–financed education violated "equal protection under the law" guarantees because the per capita amounts varied widely from district to district. With this decision, the state became the major funding source for public education.

State funding for public education has an uneven history. Between 1975 and the late 1980s, the state consistently reduced its per capita support for K–12 public education, shrinking it to 37 percent of the general fund in 1988. Amid growing concerns about weak funding and poor classroom performance, education reformers secured voter approval of **Proposition 98** in 1988, a measure that established 40 percent as a minimum funding threshold except in times of fiscal emergency. With new funds available, the state poured money into reducing class sizes in grades K–3 and lengthened the school year from 180 to 190 days. For the 2004–2005 fiscal year, schools were allocated $42.1 billion, about 43 percent of the state revenues collected through taxation, the basis of the general fund. Still, at $7,244 per student (2002–2003 figures), California expenditures remain about $600 below the national average.

Even with recent infusions, however, per capita spending has slipped to 38th–despite having one of the highest per capita incomes in the nation (Figure 8.3). California continues to be near the bottom (48th) among the states in its student–teacher ratio (a commonly used criterion for assessing education effectiveness) and in reading achievement, and California ranks 50th in the number of computers per classroom.[3] The state's graduation rate has ranked 37th for more than a decade.

Renewed focus on education has brought about improvements in some areas. Although California students were near last place in math and reading scores as recently as 1998, they have begun to make modest gains. Still, in 2003, student reading scores remained among the bottom 10 in the nation, and math scores were well below the national average. Striking disparities in education scores between those who are fluent in English and those who are not have continued.[4] With Latino and Asian American students accounting for 44 percent and 9 percent of the school

FIGURE 8.3
PERSONAL INCOME AND PUBLIC SCHOOL SPENDING IN CALIFORNIA, 1973–2004

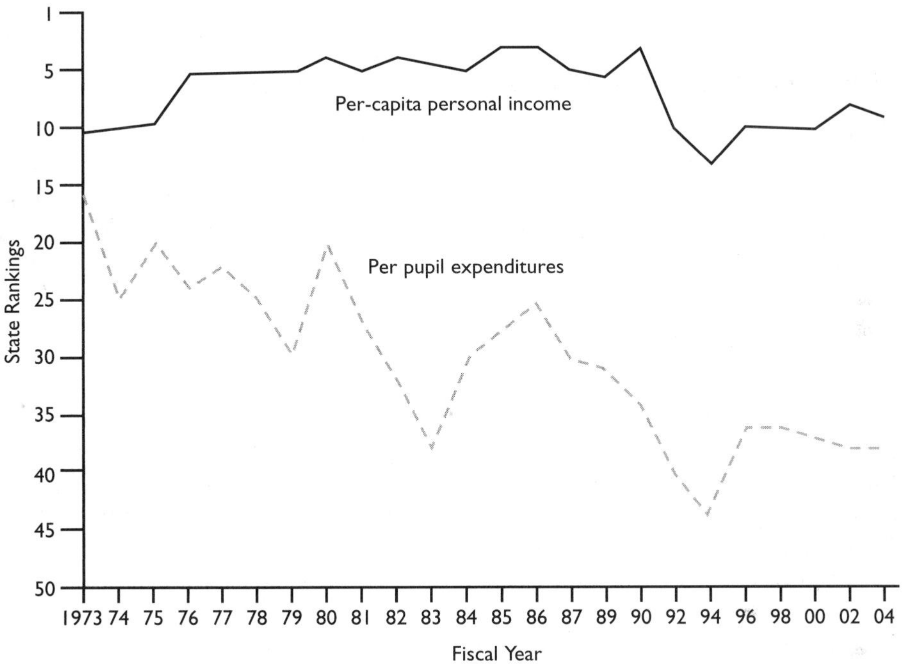

From Terry Christensen and Larry N. Gerston, *Politics in the Golden State: The California Connection,* 2nd ed., Glenview, IL: Scott Foresman, 1988, p. 203; California State Department of Education; and Bureau of Business and Economic Research, University of New Mexico.

populations, respectively, issues stemming from the language barrier can be formidable and long lasting. Passage of **Proposition 227** in 1998, a measure limiting bilingual education for non-English speaking students to one year, has added to the debate over how to "mainstream" the diverse California student community.

Nevertheless, the debate goes on. Some reformers are looking closely at "charter schools," community-controlled educational centers, as alternatives to what many describe as a broken system. As of 2004, there are about 500 charter schools in California, still a small number compared to the state's 8,700 traditional public schools. Others have promoted vouchers–cash payments for parents to select an education institution; the voters rejected such a measure in 1993 and 2000. A recent U.S.

Supreme Court decision allowing voucher programs has spawned a few of these institutions in other states.[5]

PUBLIC EDUCATION: COLLEGES AND UNIVERSITIES

Three components share responsibility for higher education in California. The state's 109 two-year community colleges enroll about 2.9 million students. Funding for these institutions is connected to the formula for primary and secondary public schools; to that extent, they have benefited from Proposition 98.

California also has two groups of 4-year public institutions. With 201,000 students, the University of California (UC) educates both undergraduate and graduate students at 10 campuses throughout the state. Designated as the state's primary research university, UC is the only public institution permitted to award professional degrees (such as medicine and law) and doctorates. The California State University (CSU) system, with 409,000 students at 23 campuses, concentrates on undergraduate instruction, awarding master's degrees most commonly in such fields as education, engineering, and business.

State support for higher education was fairly consistent until the 1990s, holding at about 11 percent of the general-fund budget, and peaked at 12.7 percent during the 2002–2003 fiscal year. Support eroded considerably during the budget crisis that followed, with the state allocation dropping to about 10 percent of the general fund in 2004–2005. More significantly, the state's share of financial support has decreased precipitously. For example, whereas California provided 82 percent of UC's education costs in 1985–1986, support dropped to 63 percent in 2002–2003. At both UC and CSU, student fees have escalated dramatically to compensate for the loss of state funds.

HEALTH AND HUMAN SERVICES

Health and human services programs receive the second-largest share of the state budget. The programs accounting for the most significant state commitment include Aid to Families with Dependent Children (AFDC), Medi-Cal, and the Supplemental Security Income (SSI) program. Medi-Cal provides health-care benefits for the poor, and SSI offers state assistance to the elderly and the disabled; but no program carries the political charge of AFDC, which is the primary recipient of the state's welfare budget.

California has sizable welfare costs. With about 12 percent of the nation's population, the state is home to 22 percent of its welfare recipients. In 1990, California had 10.5 percent of the nation's population and 12 percent of its welfare recipients.

As welfare numbers have increased, per capita spending has gone down. Changes in state policy began with Pete Wilson's administration.

Between 1991 and 1999, the average monthly state payment for a three-member family in the AFDC program dropped from $693 to $609. With new federal legislation, the state's major welfare program changed to the Temporary Assistance for Needy Families (TANF) program in 1997, which limited welfare payments to no more than 5 years.

As of 2004–2005, health and human service programs accounted for about a quarter of the general fund. Average welfare payments hovered near $700 for the typical family. Because of the 5-year limit, the state's welfare population dropped by 48 percent from 1995 to 2003.[6]

PRISONS

Among the major recipients of state allocations, the prison and corrections budgets have grown the most in recent years. As with education, the public has played a role in this policy area. In 1982, voters passed **Proposition 8**–commonly known as the Victims' Bill of Rights–an initiative that established mandatory prison terms for various crimes and extended the terms for many other crimes. Even more sweeping changes occurred in 1994, when the legislature, and later the voters, enacted a new "get tough" law commonly referred to as the "three strikes" law (as in "three strikes and you're out"). This new law required a sentence of 25 years to life for anyone convicted of three felonies.

As a result of these policy changes, California's prison population swelled beyond belief. Between 1976 and 1982, the state's prison population grew by 60 percent, from 20,000 to 32,000. After the passage of Proposition 8, the prison population jumped to 162,136 in 1999, a staggering 407-percent increase from 1982. Since 2000, the state prison population has held constant in spite of continued state growth, leading some observers to wonder whether the state's "get tough" laws have finally turned the tide. About 5.5 percent of the state's general fund was used for youth and adult corrections during the 2004–2005 fiscal year, less than in the past and now under capacity because of new parole rules. Still, California's prison budget seems to be at something of a crossroads. Experts project 15,000 fewer inmates by 2014. At the same time, the state continues work on a new prison in Delano, which will house an additional 5,000 inmates and operate at an annual cost of $110 million.[7]

MODERN STATE BUDGETS: TOO LITTLE, TOO MUCH, OR JUST RIGHT?

Have you ever met anyone who claims that he or she should pay more taxes? Neither have we. Almost everybody dislikes paying taxes, and almost everybody thinks that the money collected is spent incorrectly.

However, although most people oppose increased taxes, they also oppose program cuts. In fact, as the state surplus swelled in 2000, 67 percent of the respondents in a statewide survey said that they would prefer to use the surplus for state and local services such as education, law enforcement, and transportation, compared with 20 percent who called for a rebate.[8] Now, with the state facing annual deficits, most voters believe that the governor and legislature will have to raise taxes to keep essential services.[9]

Like their counterparts elsewhere, California policy makers have struggled to find a fair system of taxation to pay for needed programs. Given the involvement of so many public and private interests, however, fairness is difficult to determine. Moreover, during the last few decades, taxation and budget decisions have been subject to radical change. Somehow, the state's infrastructure has survived, although critics have been less than thrilled with the fiscal uncertainty that has become commonplace in California government.

Notes

1. "Debt remains in governor's budget plan," *San Jose Mercury News,* July 1, 2004, pp. 1A, 17A.
2. "Howard Jarvis Taxpayers Association," retrieved February 26, 1998, from www.hjta.org/about.htm.
3. "State and Local Source Book," *Governing,* 2004, p. 100.
4. "Stanford 9 Scores Paint a Picture of Contrasts in State," *Los Angeles Times,* July 23, 1999, pp. A1, A24.
5. In the 2002 case of *Zelman v. Simmons-Harris* (00-1751), the U.S. Supreme Court endorsed a Cleveland voucher program, leading one California expert to suggest that "it's going to add legitimacy to vouchers." See "Supreme Court, 5-4, Upholds Voucher System That Pays Religious Schools' Tuition," *The New York Times,* June 26, 2002, pp. A1, A17.
6. "Welfare numbers down, but study says many who left aren't getting by," *Monterey Herald,* January 6, 2004, p. 1.
7. "Critics say new state prison defies logic," *San Francisco Chronicle,* January 5, 2004, p. 1.
8. The Field Poll, Release #1952, February 14, 2000, p. 3.
9. The Field Poll, Release #2115, May 27, 2004, p. 2.

Learn More on the World Wide Web

California Budget Project: www.cbp.org

California state budget: www.dof.ca.gov; www.lao.ca.gov

California Taxpayers Association: www.caltax.org

National Governors' Association: www.nga.org

Learn More at the Library

David C. Nice, *Policy Innovation in State Government,* Ames: Iowa State University Press, 1994.

George R. Zodrow, *State Sales and Income Taxes: An Economic Analysis,* College Station: Texas A&M University Press, 1999.

CHAPTER 9

LOCAL GOVERNMENT: POLITICS AT THE GRASSROOTS

Citizens and the media tend to focus on state and national politics, but local government activities often have a greater impact on our daily lives. Cities, counties, and school districts make decisions that affect the traffic on our streets, the quality (and quantity) of our water, the comfort and safety of our neighborhoods, the education of our children, and the assistance available to those of us who fall on hard times. Local government is also where citizens can have their greatest influence, simply because it is closer than Sacramento or Washington, D.C.

Although local governments are accountable to the citizens they serve, they are also agencies of the state. Local governments are created by state law, which assigns them their rights and duties, mandating some functions and activities and prohibiting others. The state also allocates taxing powers and shares revenues with local governments. But the state can change the rights and powers granted to local governments at any time, expanding or reducing their tasks, funding, and independence.

COUNTIES AND CITIES

California's 58 counties and 477 cities were created in slightly different ways and perform distinctly different tasks.

COUNTIES

California is divided into **counties** (see the map inside the front cover), ranging in size from San Francisco's 49 square miles to San Bernardino County's 20,164 and in population from Alpine County, with about a thousand residents, to Los Angeles County, with over 10 million. Counties function both as local governments and as administrative units of the state. As local governments, counties provide police and fire protection, maintain roads, and perform other services for rural and unincorporated areas (those that are not part of any city). They also run jails, operate transit systems, protect health and sanitation, and keep records on property, marriages, and deaths. As agencies of the state, counties oversee elections, operate the courts, administer the state's welfare system, and collect some taxes.

The state's **general law** on counties prescribes the organization of county government. A county's central governing body is a five-member **board of supervisors,** whom voters elect by districts to staggered 4-year terms. The board sets county policies and oversees the budget, usually hiring a chief administrator or **county executive** to carry out its programs. Besides the members of the board of supervisors, the voters elect the sheriff, district attorney, tax assessor, and other department heads (Figure 9.1). Conflicts often occur as the elected board tries to manage the budget and the elected executives attempt to deliver services. Unlike most of their state counterparts, these local officials are chosen in nonpartisan elections, a Progressive legacy that keeps party labels off the ballot; all serve 4-year terms.

Although most counties operate under this general-law system, 12 have exercised a state-provided option to organize their own governmental structures through documents called **charters.** Most of these charter

FIGURE 9.1

COUNTY GOVERNMENT: AN ORGANIZATIONAL CHART FOR CALIFORNIA'S 45 GENERAL-LAW COUNTIES

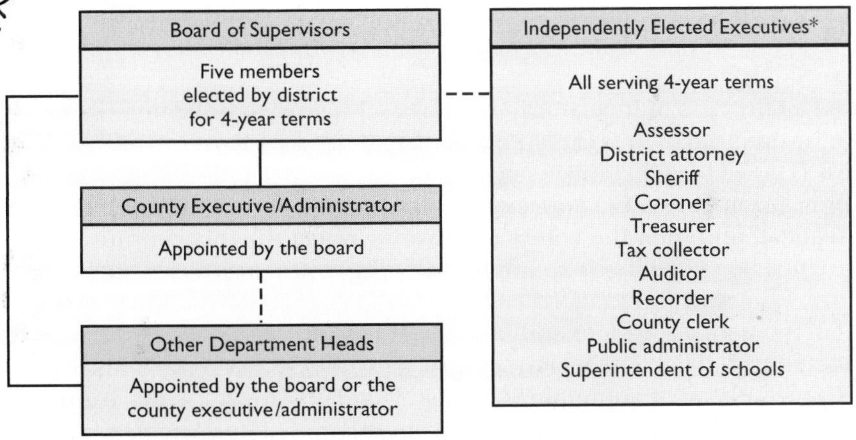

*Charter counties usually elect only the sheriff, assessor, and district attorney.

counties, including Los Angeles, Sacramento, San Diego, and Santa Clara, are highly urbanized. County voters must approve the charter and any proposed amendments. Generally, "home rule" or charter counties use their local option to replace elected county administrators with appointees of the board of supervisors or to strengthen the powers of the county executive. Voters in Los Angeles County recently used their charter authority to increase the size of their board of supervisors from five to nine to provide better representation.

San Francisco is unique among California's local governments, functioning as both a city and a county. Most counties have several cities within their boundaries, but the separate city and county governments of San Francisco were consolidated in 1911. San Francisco thus has a board of supervisors with 11 members rather than a city council, but unlike any other county, it has a mayor.

No new county has been formed in California since 1907, although in some large counties, such as Los Angeles, San Bernardino, and Santa Barbara, rural areas frustrated by urban domination have tried unsuccessfully to break away and form their own jurisdictions.

CITIES

Whereas counties are created by the state, **cities** are established at the request of their citizens, through the process of **incorporation.** As an unincorporated area urbanizes, residents begin to demand more services than the county can deliver. These may include police and fire protection, street maintenance, water, or other services. Residents may also wish to form a city to preserve the identity of their community or to avoid being annexed by some other city. Wealthy areas sometimes incorporate to protect their tax resources or their ethnic homogeneity from the impact of an adjacent big city and its economic and racial problems. California's newest city, incorporated in 2003 with a population of 29,000, is Goleta, near Santa Barbara.

The process of incorporation starts with a petition from citizens who live in the area. Then the county's **local agency formation commission** (LAFCO) determines whether the new city makes social and economic sense. If LAFCO approves, the county's board of supervisors holds a hearing, and then the voters approve or reject the incorporation.

Once formed, cities expand by annexing unincorporated (county) territory. Sometimes, small cities that can't provide adequate services disband themselves by consolidating with an adjacent city. More rarely, residents of an existing city seek to de-annex or secede. This was the case recently with some parts of Los Angeles. The 222-square-mile San Fernando Valley hosts one third of the population of Los Angeles, but many residents feel isolated and ignored by their city government. For years, they agitated to secede, and their proposal was voted on in November 2002, along with a similar proposal for secession by Hollywood. Secession required approval by the voters of both these areas and the city as a whole, however, and while the San Fernando Valley narrowly supported secession, the voters of Los Angeles and Hollywood rejected the plan. Unless the discontent of the Valley and other parts of Los Angeles is resolved, agitation for secession is likely to continue.

Like California counties, most California cities operate under the state's general law, which prescribes their governmental structure. General-law cities typically have a five-member **city council,** with members elected in nonpartisan elections for 4-year terms. The council appoints a **city manager** to supervise daily operations; the manager, in turn, appoints department heads such as the police and fire chiefs (Figure 9.2).

Cities with populations exceeding 3,500 may choose to write their own charters. A hundred and seven California cities have done so. A charter city has more discretion in choosing the structure of its government than a general-law city does. It also has more freedom to levy taxes not specifically forbidden by state law and to set policies that no state law supersedes. All of California's largest cities have their own charters to achieve greater flexibility in dealing with their complex problems.

Whether operating under general law or a home-rule charter, once incorporated, a city takes on extensive responsibilities for local services,

FIGURE 9.2

CITY GOVERNMENT: AN ORGANIZATIONAL CHART FOR CALIFORNIA'S GENERAL-LAW CITIES

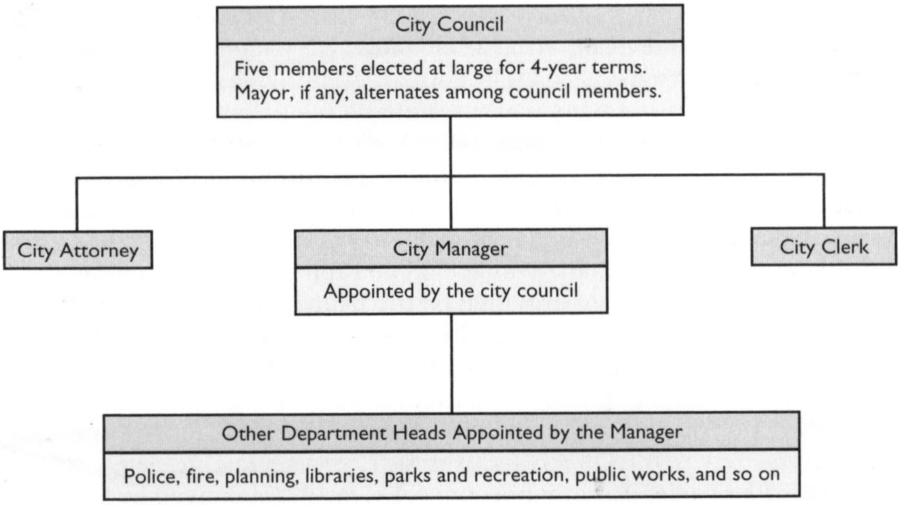

including police and fire protection, sewage treatment, garbage disposal, parks and recreational services, streets and traffic management, library operation, and land-use planning. The county, however, still provides courts, jails, welfare, elections, tax collection, public health, and public transit.

POWER IN THE CITY: COUNCIL MEMBERS, MANAGERS, AND MAYORS

Almost all of California's cities have five-member city councils with appointed city managers as executives, as set forth in the state's general law. Some cities, particularly older and larger communities, have developed municipal government structures uniquely suited to their own needs and preferences. City councils, for example, may be chosen in a variety of ways or expanded in size to allow for more representation. Los Angeles has 15 council members, San Jose 10, and San Diego 8. San Francisco's board of supervisors has 11 members. The executive office also varies among these cities; some opt for a stronger mayor rather than the manager prescribed by general law.

ELECTIONS

In most California cities, each council member is chosen by the whole city in **at-large elections.** This system was created by the Progressives to replace **district elections,** in which each council member represented only part of the city. At-large elections were intended to reduce the parochial influence of machine-organized ethnic neighborhoods on the city as a whole. The strategy worked, but as a result, ethnic minority candidates, unable to secure enough votes from other areas of the city to win at large, were rarely elected. As cities grew, citywide campaigns also became extremely costly. The Progressives added to the difficulties of minority candidates and further raised the costs of campaigns by making local elections nonpartisan. This weakened the old party machines, but voters lost the modest cue provided by the listing of parties on the ballot, minority candidates were denied the legitimization of a party label, and campaigns cost more because candidates had to get their messages out without help from a party organization.

To increase minority representation and cut campaign costs, some cities have returned to district elections. Los Angeles has used district elections since 1924; Sacramento converted in 1971, followed by San Jose, Oakland, and later San Diego and San Francisco. About two dozen

California cities use district elections. Most cities that have reverted to district elections have done so through voter-approved charter amendments, but Watsonville, a small city near Monterey, did so under a 1988 federal court ruling that at-large elections prevented Latinos from winning representation on the city council even though they constituted nearly half of the city's population.

Although district elections increased opportunities for minority candidates in some cities, minorities remain substantially underrepresented overall in California's local governments. Latinos, Asians, and African Americans constitute more than 50 percent of the state's population, but they held only 20.7, 3.2, and 4.6 percent, respectively, of the offices of mayor, council member, and county supervisor in 2001. Women have done somewhat better, with 36.9 percent (of these, a substantial number are also minorities). All these groups are more successful in local elections than in state elections, but they are still held back by discrimination, low participation, at-large elections, high campaign costs, and the lack of party support that results from nonpartisan elections.

Voter participation in local elections varies considerably from city to city. Turnout is generally higher in cities with elected mayors and district elections, but the key factor related to turnout is when the elections are held. About one third of California's cities hold their elections separate from state and national elections. Median turnout in these elections is less than 30 percent. Turnout in cities that hold their elections concurrently with state and national elections is nearly twice as high.[1] Los Angeles, for example, holds its elections separately and turnout in that city's hotly contested 2001 mayoral runoff election was 36.2 percent. Lower turnout significantly affects outcomes because the composition of the electorate changes along with the number of voters, with older, more affluent voters predominating. The Silicon Valley city of Santa Clara started holding local elections at the same time as state and national in 1988, and voter turnout went from 23–24 percent to 74 percent. Unlike cities, all of California counties hold their elections at the same time as state and national elections. Voting for local officials may still be lower, however, due to "drop-off," with some participating voters declining to cast ballots in local races because of lack of interest or information.

As with state-level campaigns, local reformers have been concerned about the costs of city and county races and the influence of money on politics. Spending on local campaigns has risen steadily since the 1980s, when professional campaign consultants and their techniques (see Chapter 3) became common in local races. One hundred and thirty-seven California cities and counties have enacted local campaign-finance laws that require disclosure of contributors and expenditures and sometimes limit the amount of contributions. These data are available online to citizens in only a few cities, however, including Los Angeles, Sacramento, and San Francisco. Los Angeles also restricts spending and provides limited public financing for campaigns. Nevertheless, in 2001, candidates for mayor of Los Angeles spent a combined total of more than $25 million in the primary and runoff elections; the winner, James Hahn, spent more than $7 million. Long Beach, Sacramento, and San Francisco are also experimenting with public financing of campaigns.[2]

EXECUTIVE POWER

Because mayors were once connected with political machines, the Progressive reformers stripped away their powers, shifting executive authority to council-appointed city managers who were intended to be neutral, professional administrators. Most California cities use this **council–manager system.** While the manager administers the city's programs, appoints department heads, and proposes the budget, the council members alternate as mayor, a ceremonial post that involves chairing meetings and cutting ribbons.

San Francisco, however, uses a strong-mayor form of government, in which the **mayor** is elected directly by the people to a 4-year term and holds powers similar to those of the president in the national system, including the veto, budget control, and appointment of department heads. Oakland switched to a strong-mayor form of government in 1998, at the same time that it elected former-governor Jerry Brown as its mayor. In Los Angeles, independent commissions ran most city departments until recently. Voters approved a new charter in 2000, enhancing the powers of the mayor by making department heads responsible to that office. Mayor James Hahn, elected in 2001, thus exercises more authority than any of his predecessors.

Other California cities have also moved away from the council–manager system of government. Some have kept their managers but have revised the system so that the mayor is directly elected and has increased authority, although he or she continues to sit as a council member. Even without much authority, being a directly elected mayor brings visibility and influence. Mayors such as San Jose's Ron Gonzales exercise substantial clout despite their limited official power.

California mayors will probably continue to grow stronger, partly because of media attention but also due to the need for leadership in the tempest of city politics. Elected officials and community groups often complain about the lack of direct accountability inherent in the city–manager form, in which the executive is somewhat insulated from the voters. Giving more authority to mayors and council members makes accountability more direct, but it may also decrease the professionalism of local government.

MORE GOVERNMENTS

Besides cities and counties, California has thousands of other, less visible local governments (Table 9.1). Created by the state or by citizens, they provide designated services and have taxing powers, mostly collecting their revenues as small portions of the property taxes paid by homeowners and businesses or by charging for their services. Yet, except for the school districts, most of us are unaware of their existence.

SCHOOL DISTRICTS AND SPECIAL DISTRICTS

In California, 983 local governments called **school districts** provide education. They are created and overseen by the state and governed by elected boards, which appoint professional educators as superintendents to oversee day-to-day operations. Except for parents and teachers, whose involvement is intense, voter participation in school elections and politics is low.

The state supplies 55 percent of the funds for schools, and the federal government provides 12 percent; most of the rest comes from local property taxes. This money is for operating expenses. Building repairs and construction of new schools are funded mostly by bonds (borrowed money paid by local taxes), which until recently required approval by a two-thirds majority of the voters. Following the Proposition 13 tax revolt, such approvals became very rare, but in 2000, voters approved lowering the percentage required for approval to 55 percent, and passing bonds became easier.

Special districts are an even more common form of local government, with no fewer than 4,748 in California. Unlike cities and counties,

TABLE 9.1
CALIFORNIA'S LOCAL GOVERNMENTS

TYPE	NUMBER
Counties	58
Cities	477
Redevelopment agencies	386
School districts	983
Special districts	4,748
TOTAL	6,652

SOURCE: California state controller.

which are "general-purpose" governments, special districts usually provide a single service. They are created when citizens or governments want a particular service performed but either have no appropriate government agency to perform the service or don't want to delegate it to a city or county. Sometimes special districts are formed when small communities share responsibilities for fire protection, sewage treatment, or other services that can be more efficiently provided on a larger scale. Depending on the nature of the special district, funding usually is by property taxes or charges for the service that it provides. The number of special districts increased when Proposition 13 imposed tax constraints on general-purpose local governments because some services can be funded more easily in this way. Altogether, California's special districts spend more than $24 billion a year, while California cities spend $39 billion and counties spend $33 billion.

A city council or a county board of supervisors governs some special districts, but most are overseen by a commission or board of directors, which may be elected or appointed by other officials. Like a school board, this body usually appoints a professional administrator to manage its business. Accountability to the voters and taxpayers is a problem, however, because most of us aren't even aware of these officials.

Like special districts, **redevelopment agencies** have also proliferated since Proposition 13 as a way for cities to raise money for special purposes without voter action. California's 386 redevelopment agencies operate within cities to provide improvements and subsidies for new projects in areas designated as "blighted" (usually old city centers and industrial areas). New property tax revenues generated by redevelopment must be reinvested in the redevelopment areas, enabling cities to make infrastructure improvements and build housing and public facilities such as convention centers. As with special districts, accountability is a problem with redevelopment agencies. Although such agencies are technically separate from city government, the local city council generally acts as the agency's board of directors, although this is not the role for which council members are elected, nor is it often discussed in campaigns. Critics also charge that redevelopment agencies divert taxes from other services and hurt the low-income and minority residents of areas that are designated as "blighted."

REGIONAL GOVERNMENTS

The existence of so many sorts of local governments means that many operate in every urban region of California. The vast urban areas between Los Angeles and San Diego or San Francisco and San Jose, for example, consist of many cities, counties, and special districts, with no single authority in charge of the whole area. This fragmentation creates small-scale governments that are accessible to citizens, but these governments are sometimes too small to provide the needed services efficiently. In addition, problems such as transportation and air pollution go far beyond the boundaries of any one entity.

Many California cities deal with this situation by contracting for services from counties, larger cities, or private businesses. The 88 cities of Los Angeles County, for example, may pay the county to provide any of 58 different services, from dog catching to tree planting. Small cities commonly contract with the county sheriff for police protection rather than fund their own forces. Contracting allows such communities to provide needed services while retaining local control, although some see the system as unfair because wealthy communities can afford more than poor ones.

Special districts are another way to deal with regional problems, particularly those extending beyond the boundaries of existing cities or counties, such as air pollution and transportation. California has 47 transit districts, for example, which run bus and rail systems. Most are countywide, but some, such as the Bay Area Rapid Transit (BART) system, cover several counties.

Twenty of California's urban areas also have **councils of government (COGs),** in which all of the cities and counties in each area are represented. The biggest COGs are the six-county Southern California Association of Governments (SCAG) and the nine-county Association of Bay Area Governments (ABAG) in Northern California. These regional bodies focus on land-use planning and development, but because they cannot force their plans on local governments, they serve mainly as forums for communication and coordination among the jurisdictions they encompass.

As regional problems have grown and competition among cities has increased, the need for regional planning has also grown. The state has asserted its authority over local governments to require the implementation of regional plans through agencies such as ABAG and ASCG. Other state-created agencies, such as the Metropolitan Water District and the South Coast Air Quality Management Board in Southern California, exercise great power. Environmentalists, big business, and metropolitan newspapers often advocate the creation of regional governments with the ability to deal with areawide issues such as transportation, air quality, and growth, but existing cities firmly oppose any loss of local control.

DIRECT DEMOCRACY IN LOCAL POLITICS

Direct democracy is used even more locally than statewide, with 470 city and county measures on the ballot in November 2002 alone. All charter changes, such as increasing the powers of the mayor or introducing district council elections, are subject to voter approval by referendum. Voters must also approve proposals for local governments to introduce or raise taxes or to borrow money by issuing bonds. Charter changes require a simple majority, but a supermajority of two thirds is required for most taxes. Resulting from a series of statewide initiatives, these requirements have severely restricted the ability of local governments to raise money because voter approval is difficult to win.

Local governments can place tax measures and charter amendments on the ballot, but citizens also put proposals to the voters through the initiative process. Citizens have commonly done so to control growth and amend charters. District elections were introduced in some cities by initiative, as were **term limits,** usually restricting elected officials to two 4-year terms. Several California counties and about 40 cities now limit the terms of elected officials. As a last resort, voters may express their dissatisfaction with elected officials through recall elections. Recalls are rare, occurring mostly in school districts, but threats of recall became more common after the successful recall of Governor Gray Davis in 2003.

LAND USE: COPING WITH GROWTH

The most frequent use of direct democracy in California cities and counties is by citizens seeking to control growth. Deciding how land can be used is a major power assigned to local governments by the state. The way they use this power affects us all. If they encourage growth in the form of housing, industry, or shopping centers, for example, the economy may boom, but streets may become clogged, schools overcrowded, sewage treatment plants strained, and police and fire protection stretched too thin. When this happens, environmentalists or residents who expect adequate services may grow frustrated and demand controls on growth. If the city council or county board of supervisors is unresponsive, they may take their case to the voters through an initiative.

Since 1971, when development became the state's predominant local issue, 90 percent of California communities have enacted some form of growth control, and growth-related measures continue to appear on local ballots throughout the state. Several communities in fast-growing Ventura County have recently approved strict controls. The battle typically pits a grassroots coalition with little money against big-spending developers and builders. The antigrowth faction usually wins, but sometimes those who favor development persuasively emphasize the economic benefits of growth, including jobs and housing. Voters in Orange County, Riverside County, and San Diego recently rejected growth-control measures, despite dissatisfaction with the local quality of life. Statewide surveys report that voter support for local growth control initiatives declined from 58 percent in 2000 to 49 percent in 2002.[3]

TAXING AND SPENDING

The way that local governments raise and spend money reveals a great deal, not only about what they do but also about the limits they face in doing it.

The biggest single source of money for California's local governments used to be the **property tax,** an annual assessment based on the value of land and buildings. Then, in 1978, the voters approved **Proposition 13,** a statewide initiative that cut property tax revenues by 57 percent. Cities adjusted to Proposition 13 in a variety of ways. Some cut jobs and services to save money. Many introduced or increased **charges for services** such as sewage treatment, trash collection, building permits, and the use of recreational facilities. Such charges are now the largest source of income for most cities (Figure 9.3), followed by the **sales tax,** which returns .75 percent of the state's basic 7.25-percent sales tax to the city where the sale occurred (or the county, in the case of unincorporated areas). Another .5 percent of the sales tax goes to local governments for public safety, and counties get .75 percent for transportation. Some counties add to the basic tax to obtain further funds for transportation, but they cannot exceed the 9-percent maximum sales tax set by the state.

Utility taxes also help some cities, such as San Jose, where they comprise 15 percent of local revenues, almost as much as property taxes. The shift from property taxes to other sources of revenue also affected local land-use decisions. When a new development is proposed, most cities now prefer retail businesses to housing or industry because of the sales taxes that such businesses generate. This trend has been labeled the **fiscalization of land use** because instead of choosing the best use for the land, cities opt for the one that produces the most revenue.

With more legal constraints on their taxing powers, counties had an even rougher time after Proposition 13. State aid to counties increased slightly, but with no alternative local taxes readily available after the passage of Proposition 13, most counties cut spending deeply. Years later, they are still struggling to provide essential services. Like cities, most counties increased charges and fees for services. Orange County, for example, approved California's first toll road in half a century when it couldn't afford to build a new freeway. Orange County was also nearly bankrupted when its county treasurer tried to make money for the county by using funds on hand to play the stock market and instead lost disastrously.

More than half of county revenues come from the state and federal governments (40.7 percent and 22.5 percent, respectively), but this money

FIGURE 9.3

Revenues and Expenditures of California Cities and Counties, 2001–2002

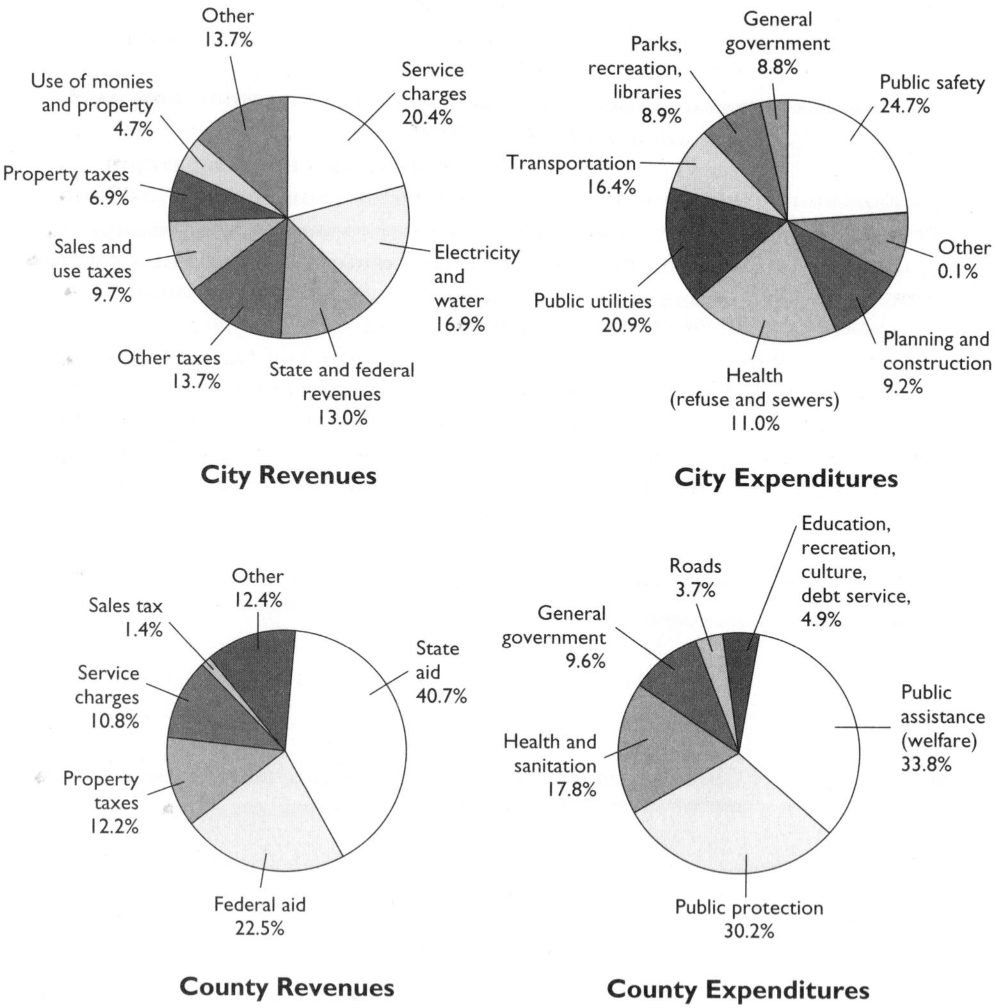

SOURCE: California state controller, 2004.

must be spent on required programs and institutions such as welfare, medical assistance, and the courts. Even so, state and federal aid does not cover the cost of these mandatory services, leaving counties with little money to spend as they choose. The average California county spends 95 percent of its funds on state-mandated services, compared with 70 percent 15 years ago.[4]

Just as the revenue sources of cities and counties differ, so do their spending patterns, largely because the state assigns them different responsibilities. As Figure 9.3 shows, public safety is the biggest expenditure for California cities, whereas welfare is the biggest county expenditure.

The revenues and expenditures of both cities and counties have been increasingly constrained by the state during recent budget crises. In the 1990s, the state shifted property tax funds from cities and counties to schools and did so again in 2004, when local governments also lost much of their income from vehicle license fees and the state took property tax revenues from redevelopment agencies to balance its budget. Cities were so frustrated by all this that they pushed for a constitutional amendment to "lock in" their revenues. During negotiations on the 2004–2005 budget, the cities and counties cut a deal with Governor Schwarzenegger, agreeing to accept a $1.3-billion reduction in their revenues in return for a promise that the governor would support a constitutional amendment to guarantee future revenues and prevent such state "take backs." Voters approved **Proposition 1A** in November 2004, thus providing local governments with greater financial security in the future.

LOCAL LIMITS

California's political system gives residents of cities and counties many opportunities to decide what sort of communities they want, and Californians make good use of these opportunities. But the state also limits what can be done at the local level, as Proposition 13 and ongoing budget battles clearly show. These limits are not only fiscal, however. The state delegates the authority to issue marriage licenses to counties, for example, but when the city and county of San Francisco started issuing marriage licenses to same-sex couples in 2004, the courts ruled that such marriages contravened state law and halted the licensing. Some may dispute such interventions, but the state's authority remains supreme.

Notes

1. Zoltan L. Hajnal, Paul G. Lewis, and Hugh Louch, "Municipal Elections in California: Turnout, Timing, and Competition," Public Policy Institute of California (www.ppic.org), March 2002.

2. "Public Financing Laws in Local Jurisdictions," Center for Government Studies (www.cgs.org), October 27, 2003.
3. "PPIC Statewide Survey," Public Policy Institute of California (www.ppic.org), March 2000 and June 2002.
4. County Supervisors Association of California.

Learn More on the World Wide Web

Association of (San Francisco) Bay Area Governments: www.abag.org

Cities: www.cacities.org

Counties: www.csac.counties.org

Data on cities, counties, schools, and special districts: www.sco.ca.gov

Public Policy Institute of California (studies on local government): www.ppic.org

Southern California Association of Governments: www.scag.ca.gov

Learn More at the Library

Jeffrey I. Chapman, *Proposition 13: Some Unintended Consequences,* San Francisco: Public Policy Institute of California, 1998.

Paul G. Lewis, *Deep Roots: Local Government Structure in California,* San Francisco: Public Policy Institute of California, 1998.

Peter Schrag, *Paradise Lost,* Berkeley: University of California Press, 1999.

CHAPTER 10

STATE-FEDERAL RELATIONS: CONFLICT, COOPERATION, AND CHAOS

Part of California's uniqueness stems from its position as the nation's most populated state; part also stems from the state's vast resources, size, and diversity. Problems and achievements occur in proportions here that are unequaled elsewhere. And so it is regarding the state's relationship with the federal government.

Sometimes state and national leaders differ in opinion about how California should be managed. Environmental protection and government regulation of electricity prices are two such thorny policy areas. On other issues, such as workplace conditions and foreign trade, the two governments have worked well together. Deciding the best responses to problems that impact both the nation and state can be a challenge because, like its 49 counterparts, California is both a self-governing state and member of the larger national government.

Matters become even more complicated when attempts are made to determine financial responsibility for new highways, immigration control, or homeland security, to name a few. Because the state is so large and complex, federal assistance almost always seems inadequate. Yet, when federal aid or programs are cut, California seems to suffer disproportionately.

Nevertheless, when the state succeeds, its attainment is often the harbinger of similar good fortune destined to reach the rest of the nation. The right-to-choose movement, environmentalism, gun control, political reform, the tax revolt, and gay marriage all had early beginnings–and in some cases, origins–in California.

In this chapter, we review California's impact on national policy making and policy actors. We also explore some of the critical policy areas that test California's relationship with the federal government: immigration, the environment, and the distribution of federal resources to the state of California. Each issue touches on the delicate balance between state autonomy and national objectives–perspectives that are not always shared. These issues are important not only because of their present urgency, but also because of their effects on California's people, economy, and political values.

CALIFORNIA'S CLOUT WITH THE PRESIDENT

California has had an uneven relationship with the nation's presidents over the past decade. During his 8 years in office, Democratic President Bill Clinton embraced the state. Keenly aware of the state's growing wealth and the value of California's 55 electoral votes (20 percent of the electoral college votes needed to win the presidency), he funneled discretionary funds to California, particularly in the areas of high-tech research and defense industry projects. Clinton was also pro-choice, pro-gun control, and environmentally sensitive–themes that resonate with most Californians. None of this was lost on the California electorate, which supported Democratic Vice President Al Gore in 2000 over the winner, Republican George W. Bush.

During his first term, Bush did not tend to California with the zeal of his predecessor. To the contrary, the Bush administration ignored California when the state sought relief from the Federal Regulatory Energy Commission over excessive electricity prices in 2001. Other fights have occurred over air pollution, agriculture, and international trade. And still unresolved is the extent to which the federal government will help California with its bills for fighting terrorism. Even the election of Arnold Schwarzenegger did little to cement relations with fellow Republican and President George W. Bush except in the most cosmetic fashion. Given the clash of cultural and political values between most Californians and the conservative president, it's easy to see why the distance between the state and the president was more than a matter of miles.

CALIFORNIA'S CLOUT WITH CONGRESS

As the nation's most populated state, California has 53 members in the House of Representatives, dwarfing the delegation of every other state; Texas and New York are second and third, with 31 and 30 members, respectively. However, in congressional politics, the sizes of state delegations matter little. Rather, the majority political party in each house of Congress chooses committee chairs who, in turn, control the flow of legislation. Seniority is key to gaining chairmanships in Congress. Although Republicans have held the majority in the House of Representatives since 1995, only in recent years have members from California assumed key positions, thanks in part to a Republican rule restricting chairmanships to 6 years. Thus, during the 108th Congress (2003–2005), Californians held 5 of the 21 committee chairmanships.[1] Ohio is next with three chairmanships, followed by Florida, Illinois, and Virginia with two each. On the Democratic side, in 2002 San Francisco Congresswoman Nancy Pelosi won election to the post of minority leader, making her the most powerful Democrat in the House. Pelosi's post is also the highest national leadership position ever held by a woman.

Matters are somewhat different in the U.S. Senate. Although the upper house is a bit less partisan than the lower house, the majority party still controls all committees. Democrats held a slim majority until 2002, when Republicans took over. The switch left California's two Democratic senators, Dianne Feinstein and Barbara Boxer, removed from the center of power, although they still exercise considerable influence over issues such as energy, judicial appointments, and environmental policy.

INTERNAL COMPOSITION

In many respects California's congressional makeup is as diverse as the rest of the state. As of 2005, the 53-member House delegation includes 7 Latinos, 4 African Americans, and 2 Asians; 18 women are members of the delegation. Both of California's U.S. senators are women as well.

Unlike the overall composition of the House of Representatives, Democrats in California now enjoy a comfortable margin of 33–20 over Republicans. The re-election of Democrat Barbara Boxer in 2004 kept both of the state's senate seats in the Democratic camp, contrary to the national Republican majority.

DIVISIVENESS

One other fact must be added to the discussion of Californians in Washington–historically, the state's **congressional delegation** has been notoriously fractured in its responses to key public policy issues affecting California. Much of the conflict stems from the makeup of their districts. North/south, urban/rural, and coastal/valley/mountain divisions separate the state geographically. Other differences exist, too, in terms of wealth, ethnicity, and basic liberal/conservative distinctions. To be sure, no congressional district is completely homogenous, yet most members of Congress tend to protect their districts' interests more than those of the state as a whole. Thus, on issues ranging from desert protection to immigration, representatives have often canceled each other's votes, leaving states such as Texas far more powerful because of their relatively unified stances. Even on foreign trade issues, members from California often have worked at cross-purposes, depending on the industries, interest groups, and demographic characteristics of their districts. Only on the question of offshore oil drilling have most members of the state's delegation voted the same way.

The struggle over the proposed Auburn Dam is a current case in point. The massive $2.6-billion proposal has been considered in Congress since 1960, yet California lawmakers in Washington have remained paralyzed over the issue. Republican John Doolittle, a member of the House Appropriations Committee, and Sacramento Democrat Bob Matsui, a senior member of the Ways and Means Committee, have pushed the project, but Democrats Pete Stark and George Miller have adamantly opposed it. The issue of whether the project is a boondoggle or a necessary flood-control program is not as significant as the fact that it has polarized California members of the House of Representatives. As a result, while Californians have fussed among themselves over this polarizing question, representatives from other states have worked in bipartisan ways to garner federal dollars.

TERRORISM

September 11, 2001, represented a turning point in American history. Never before had terrorists penetrated American soil in such a punishing way. As expected, the federal government took the lead in responding to this unprecedented event. With passage of the USA Patriot Act on October 26, 2001, the national government assumed expanded powers to search out terrorism and terrorist-related activities in the areas of hazardous substances, money laundering, illegal immigration, cybercrime, fraud, and other related areas. Acting in concert with these new powers, U.S. Attorney General John Ashcroft asked states and local governments to help in detaining and questioning suspicious persons; the new Transportation Security Administration assumed security responsibilities at the nation's airports; and the U.S. Border Patrol increased its vigilance against illegal entry.

Although the federal government has picked up some of the tab, the states have been burdened with significant costs, too, and are likely to see those costs continue well into the future. From bus transportation systems to water transportation conduits, California's infrastructure now requires additional protection against terrorists. Statewide, former California Highway Patrol Commissioner D. O. "Spike" Helmick estimated in 2002 that law enforcement costs would increase by a staggering $2 billion annually.[2] Such costs are difficult for governments to swallow in good economic times, but with the state plagued by a lingering recession between 2002 and 2004, they made a major dent in depleted resources.

Even the state's new surge in congressional chairmanships does not seem to have helped California's position with the federal government. The struggle over federal funds for homeland security is a current example. Following the September 11 terrorist attacks on the United States, the federal government has made antiterrorism funds available to all 50 states. With $5.03 per capita for the 2004–2005 fiscal year, California ranks last, despite its 1,000-mile coastline, huge seaports, massive power line grids, and other targets that are ripe for terrorist attacks. Meanwhile, Wyoming ranked first with $37.94 per capita, followed by Vermont ($31.56 per capita), North Dakota ($30.81 per capita), and Alaska ($30.42 per capita). This occurred despite the fact that Californian Christopher Cox chairs the House Homeland Security Committee.[3]

IMMIGRATION

California has long been a magnet for those in search of opportunity. And they have come–first the Spanish, then the Yankees, the Irish, and the Chinese during the nineteenth century, followed by Japanese, Eastern Europeans, African Americans, Vietnamese beginning in the 1970s, Asian Indians in the 1990s, and more Latinos throughout the last half century. But over the past two decades, several independent events have converged to influence the moods of the state's residents and would-be residents. Lack of opportunity in other nations has led millions to choose California as an alternative; meanwhile, an overburdened and underfunded infrastructure has led many of those already here to oppose further immigration. Much of the antipathy has been directed at Latinos, but anger has also been aimed at Asians.

The numbers involved are substantial. Whereas 15.1 percent of California's population was foreign-born in 1980, 28 percent fell within that category in 2002. During the same period, the percentage of foreign-born occupants of the United States as a whole edged up from 6.2 to 12 (Figure 10.1). Between 1990 and 1999, California's population grew by between 500,000 and 600,000 annually, more than 40 percent of which came from foreign immigration. In 2003, the federal government's Census Bureau estimated that there were between 8 million and 10 million illegal immigrants nationwide, with at least 3 million of them in California.[4]

As these dramatic events began to reshape California, experts argued about whether the immigrants helped or harmed the state's economy. One study claimed that within a 3-month period, immigrants–legal and illegal–cost the state $18 billion in services; another study countered that immigrants–legal and illegal–contributed a net increase of $12 billion in taxes to California's economy.[5] These studies underscore the anguish and confusion associated with the immigration issue.

However, the largest issue related to immigration lies in determining which level of government should assume responsibility for its costs. While the federal government has long established the criteria for immigration and the conditions for enforcement, it leaves the states responsible

FIGURE 10.1
Population of Foreign-Born Residents, California and United States Compared

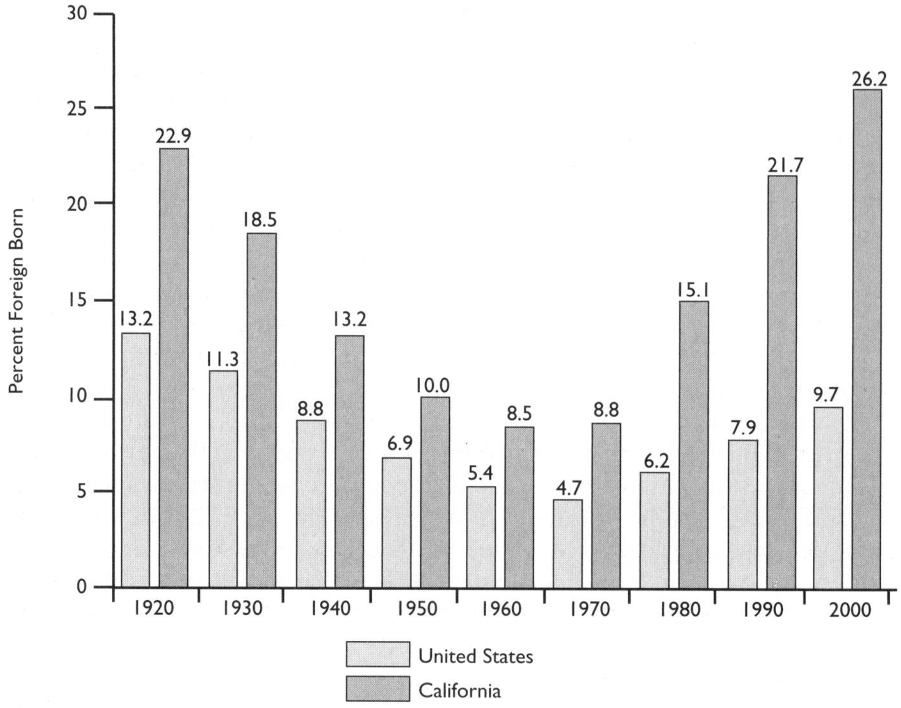

SOURCE: U.S. Census Bureau.

for meeting the needs of immigrants. Nowhere does this contradiction ring louder than in California. Among illegal immigrants alone, recent estimates cite health-care costs of $1 billion, education costs of 400,000 illegal immigrant children at $1 billion, and incarceration costs for 18,000 illegal immigrants at $500 million.[6] Few of these costs have been picked up by the federal government, yet their day-to-day management is a reality.

AIR POLLUTION

Some public policies in California emerge more from federal pressure than from state will. No example is more obvious than environmental protection, particularly as it pertains to clean air. According to the 1990

Clean Air Act amendments, five of the seven most polluted areas in the entire country lie in California; nevertheless, considerable opposition to antipollution activity has existed because of the massive costs associated with environmental repair and fears that those costs would lead to economic disaster. This dilemma has pitted Californians against Washington, D.C., and also against each other, especially Northern versus Southern California interests.

The road to consensus has been bumpy, in part because the state of California and the federal government each claim jurisdiction over air and water. At times, the federal government has deferred to California's pleas that federal standards would strangle Southern California companies as well as their automobile-dependent workforce. At other times, the federal government's **Environmental Protection Agency** (EPA) has urged, prodded, and threatened the state into compliance with fundamental national objectives. At still other times, the federal government has discouraged the state from innovation, such as in 2002 when the Bush administration joined in a suit to keep California from imposing auto emissions standards that were stronger than in other states.

Nowhere have the choices been more difficult than with air pollution in Southern California, home to much of the state's pollution-emitting industry and dirty air. For years, the South Coast Air Quality Management District, California's major environmental agency in the area, has struggled to enforce federal rules without harming the economy. Although emissions have been reduced considerably by the agency's efforts, they must be pared by another 60 percent before 2010 to comply with federal standards. Failure to meet this deadline will result in huge federal fines and the possible shutdown of local industries. In 1999, business representatives and the state and the federal government agreed on 12 rules that businesses must follow to eliminate as much as 48 tons of pollution per day. In 2002, the EPA and state came to terms on a plan to reduce vehicle smog emissions, thereby freeing $716 million of federal aid for highway projects that had been frozen during the dispute.[7]

Matters have not been resolved as easily in the Central Valley, however. In 2002, the EPA announced an end to an exemption for California farmers who had been allowed to operate heavy farm machinery outside the emissions rules. The EPA took the new stand because of the extraordinarily high percentages of children in the area suffering from asthma, thought to be caused by the area's growing air pollution. Farmers' groups claimed that they would be forced out of business, but health organizations hailed the decision.[8]

Along the winding road to environmentalism, the state has invented necessary compromises, such as a "smog exchange" program that allows polluters to "buy" sulfur oxides, hydrocarbons, and other emissions from companies that stay below their allowed pollution levels. This law drew the wrath of environmentalists. In 2002, California legislators also passed landmark legislation requiring automakers to significantly reduce greenhouse gasses from cars, trucks, minivans, and sport-utility vehicles by 2009. This law drew the wrath of businesses. Simply put, there is no easy way for the state to deal with the issue of air pollution.

WATER

Not all of California's jurisdictional disputes have occurred with the federal government. In several areas, the state has tangled with other states. The storage of nuclear waste and agriculture rules are two such examples of state fights, but no argument has as much significance as California's struggle for fresh water. Given the state's huge population and pivotal role in agriculture, water is a resource that California can ill-afford to do without.

The linchpin of the water dispute between California and other states is the Colorado River, the fresh water source that begins in Colorado and winds through six other states. Under a 1922 multistate agreement, California is entitled to 4.4 million acre-feet, or 59 percent, of the lower basin river annually. Yet, according to some critics, California has exceeded its share by as much as 1 million acre-feet per year,[9] a condition that has become problematic due to dramatic population growth in Arizona and Nevada.

Fearing an all-out water war that would spill into Congress, officials from seven states held talks for 18 months to resolve the problem. In 2000, they agreed to a formula that would allow California to gradually reduce its consumption of the excess over a 15-year period. During the transition, officials from Arizona have offered to "bank" surplus water for California, should the state require it. At least for the time being, the seven western states have solved a thorny issue without federal participation.

Meanwhile, the federal government's Department of the Interior and the state worked to resolve the ongoing battle among agribusiness, which uses 80 percent of the state's water, environmentalists seeking to preserve rivers and deltas, and urban areas in need of water to grow. Under the auspices of CalFed, a joint federal and state water agency, the two governments developed a plan in 2000 to expand existing federal reservoirs in California, improve drinking water quality, and develop a creative water recycling program. Most of the $8.5 billion price tag will be borne by the federal government, with Californians providing $825 million from the passage of Proposition 50 in 2002.

Issues still remain. In 2002, the federal Department of the Interior modified a plan previously favored by environmentalists to send more water from the Central Valley Project to farmers, rather than using it for ecosystem restoration. Then, in a rare bipartisan effort among California's congressional delegation, a bill coauthored by Democratic U.S. Senator Dianne Feinstein and Republican Ken Calvert authorized $800 million in federal funds for new water projects and stream projection. Whether all sides are satisfied remains to be seen.

SHARED RESOURCES

The word **federalism** refers to the multifaceted political relationship that binds the state and national governments. One aspect of that relationship centers on financial assistance that wends its way from federal coffers to state treasuries. The preponderance of this assistance comes in the form of **grants-in-aid,** amounting to more than $293 billion in 2000 and, on average, amounting to about 22 percent of all state and local government revenues. This assistance is the result of more than 500 federal programs designed to assist states in areas ranging from agricultural development to high-tech research. For decades, California received more than its fair share of grants-in-aid from the federal government. With defense- and space-related research serving as a huge economic magnet, the Golden State received more money from the federal government than it sent in.

That has changed. In 1981, California had 10 percent of the national population but received 15 percent of the national government's expenditures. By 1983, the federal share had jumped to 22 percent. Then came the slide. With a pared defense budget, cutbacks in infrastructure work, and the push for a balanced budget, federal contributions have shrunk considerably. As of 2002, California had 12.5 percent of the nation's population but received 11.8 percent of the nation's federal funds. The state now ranks 40th on a per capita basis among federal grant-in-aid recipients, down sharply from 20th in 1990.[10]

There is another way to appreciate the changing relationship between the federal government and California. Because of the state's massive growth and receipt of federal assistance in highway and water projects and environmental protection, California had a long history of getting more dollars from the federal government than it contributes. Beginning in 1986, however, California became a "donor" state. Ever since, California has contributed more money to the national treasury than it has received, and the disparity is increasing every year. In 1992, for every dollar California sent to Washington, D.C., the state received 88 cents in federal goods and services. In 2002, for every dollar California sent to Washington, only 76 cents came back in goods and services, leaving the state in 45th place in per capita federal spending.

But there is more to the story than just numbers; it's the kind of numbers that makes a huge difference. With respect to poverty, for example, California's poor population is a full percentage point above the national

TABLE 10.1
Federal Expenditures per Dollar of Taxes, Fiscal Years 1992 and 2002—California and Selected States

	Expenditures per Dollar of Taxes		Ranking	
	FY 1992	FY 2002	FY 1992	FY 2002
New Mexico	$2.08	$2.37	1	1
Kansas	$1.05	$1.13	27	25
Texas	$.93	$.92	37	36
California	$.93	$.76	38	45
Massachusetts	$1.01	$.75	31	46
New Jersey	$.66	$.62	50	50

SOURCE: Tax Foundation.

average.[11] Add that to the fact that the state's immigrant population is more than twice the national average on a per capita basis and it becomes clear that the state's needs fare particularly poorly when it comes to federal funding.

The data presented here fly in the face of the political posturing that has emerged from both Congress and the presidency in recent years. They are also a reflection of the fragmentation that has haunted the state's congressional delegation on virtually every issue except offshore oil drilling. As a result, California's "Golden State" nickname has a different meaning in Washington than in California–namely, sizable economic resources that have landed disproportionately in the federal treasury.

CHANGED RULES, NEW DIRECTIONS

As national leaders have altered the course of U.S. politics and public policies, their efforts have been felt profoundly in California. The state's fragmented congressional delegation and a Republican-led Congress have only exacerbated California's inability to be heard, despite the handful of chairmanships controlled by Californians in the House. And despite the election of Republican Arnold Schwarzenegger as governor, the administration of fellow Republican George W. Bush has not been helpful in responding to the state's many needs.

Still, there's another way to consider recent developments: California has been weaned from much of its dependence on federal dollars. The process may not have been enjoyable, but the state now is more diversified as a result.

Notes

1. The House of Representatives chairs and their committees are as follows: Duncan Hunter (Armed Services), Richard Pombo (Resources), David Dreier (Rules), Bill Thomas (Ways and Means), and Christopher Cox (Homeland Security).
2. "Mounting Costs Worry Safety Agencies," *Sacramento Bee,* November 16, 2001, p. 1A.
3. Source: Department of Homeland Security, Office of Domestic Preparedness, Fiscal Year 2004, November 3, 2003.
4. "Imagining Life Without Legal Immigrants," *The New York Times,* January 11, 2004, p. 1.
5. "1992 Cost of Immigrants $18 Billion, Report Says," *Los Angeles Times,* November 5, 1993, pp. A3, A31; and "Immigrants Found a Fiscal Plus," *Los Angeles Times,* February 23, 1994, p. B4.
6. These data are cited in Bernard L. Hyink and David H. Provost, *Politics and Government in California,* 16th ed., New York: Pearson Longman Publishers, 2004, p. 233.
7. "EPA Accepts Bay Area Smog Plans," *San Francisco Chronicle,* July 15, 2002, p. A23.
8. "U.S. Plans to End Exemption of California Farmers From Air Pollution Standards," *The New York Times,* May 15, 2002, p. A15.
9. "Western States Blast California Over Water Use," *Las Vegas Review-Journal,* May 22, 1999, p. 5b. The six states in addition to California are Arizona, Colorado, Nevada, New Mexico, Utah, and Wyoming.
10. Institute for Federal Policy Research, "California's Balance of Payments with the Federal Treasury, 1981–2000," April 2002.
11. Tim Ransdell, *Factors Determining California's Share of Formula Grants,* 2nd ed., San Francisco: Public Policy Institute of California, 2004, pp. 7–10.

Learn More on the World Wide Web

California and federal taxes: www.taxfoundation.org

California taxes: www.caltax.org

Environmental Protection Agency: www.epa.gov

Immigration: www.ccir.net and www.irps.ucsd.edu

Sierra Club: www.sierraclub.org

U.S. House of Representatives: www.house.gov

U.S. Senate: www.senate.gov

Learn More at the Library

Governing, 2004 State and Local Source Book. Rankings of states on taxes, expenditures and more.

Michael E. Kraft, *Environmental Policy and Politics,* 3rd ed., White Plains, NY: Longman Publishers, 2003.

Joseph Nevins, *Operation Gatekeeper: The Rise of the Illegal Alien and the Remaking of the U.S.-Mexican Boundary,* New York: Routledge, 2002.

GLOSSARY

absentee ballots Voters who prefer not to vote at their polling places or who are unable to vote on election day may apply to their county registrar of voters for an absentee ballot and vote by mail.

at-large elections Local elections in which all candidates are elected by the community as a whole rather than by districts.

attorney general California's top law-enforcement officer and legal counsel; the second-most powerful member of the executive branch.

bank and corporation tax Tax on the profits of lending institutions and businesses; the third-most important source of state revenue.

bicameral legislature Organization of the state legislature into two houses, the 40-member senate (elected for 4-year terms) and the 80-member assembly (elected for 2-year terms).

Big Five The governor, assembly speaker, assembly minority leader, senate president pro tem, and senate minority leader, who gather informally to thrash out decisions on the annual budget and other major policy issues.

Board of Equalization Five-member state board that oversees the collection of sales, gasoline, and liquor taxes; members are elected by district; part of the executive branch.

board of supervisors Five-member governing body of counties, usually elected by district to 4-year terms.

central committees Political party organizations at county and state levels; weakly linked to one another.

charges for services Local government fees for services such as sewage treatment, trash collection, building permits, and the use of recreational facilities; a major source of income for cities and counties since the passage of Proposition 13 in 1978.

charter A document defining the powers and institutions of a California city or county.

cities Local governments in urban areas, run by city councils and mayors or city managers; principal responsibilities include police and fire protection, land-use planning, street maintenance and construction, sanitation, libraries, and parks.

city councils Governing bodies of cities; members are elected at-large or by district to 4-year terms.

city manager Top administrative officer in most California cities; appointed by the city council.

civil service System for hiring and retaining public employees on the basis of their qualifications or merit; replaced the political machine's patronage, or spoils, system; encompasses 98 percent of state workers.

closed primary Election of party nominees in which only party members may participate.

collegiality Deferential behavior among justices as a way of building consensus on issues before the court.

Commission on Judicial Appointments Commission to review the governor's nominees for appellate and supreme courts; consists of the attorney general, the chief justice of the state supreme court, and the senior presiding judge of the courts of appeal.

Commission on Judicial Performance State board empowered to investigate charges of judicial misconduct or incompetence.

conference committee Committee of senate and assembly members that meets to reconcile different versions of the same bill.

congressional delegation Members of the House of Representatives and Senate representing a particular state.

contract lobbyist Individual or company that represents the interests of clients before the legislature and other policy-making entities.

controller Independently elected state executive who oversees taxing and spending.

council–manager system Form of government in which an elected council appoints a professional manager to administer daily operations; used by most California cities.

councils of government (COGs) Regional planning organizations.

counties Local governments and administrative agencies of the state, run by elected boards of supervisors; principal responsibilities include welfare, jails, courts, roads, and elections.

county executive Top administrative officer in most California counties; appointed by the board of supervisors.

courts of appeal Three-justice panels that hear appeals from lower courts.

cross-filing Election system that allowed candidates to win the nomination of more than one political party; eliminated in 1959.

demographic groups Interest groups based on race, ethnicity, gender, or age; usually concerned with overcoming discrimination.

direct democracy Progressive reforms giving citizens the power to make and repeal laws (initiative and referendum) and to remove elected officials from office (recall).

direct mail Modern campaign technique by which candidates communicate selected messages to selected voters by mail.

director of finance State officer primarily responsible for preparation of the budget; appointed by the governor.

district attorney Chief prosecuting officer elected in each county; represents the people in cases against the accused.

district elections Elections in which candidates are chosen by only one part of the city, county, or state.

Environmental Protection Agency Federal government body charged with carrying out national environmental policy objectives.

executive order The ability of the governor to make rules that have the effect of laws; may be overturned by the legislature.

Fair Political Practices Commission (FPPC) Established by the Political Reform Act of 1974, this independent regulatory commission monitors candidates' campaign finance reports and lobbyists.

federalism The distribution of power, resources, and responsibilities among the national, state, and local governments.

fiscalization of land use When making land-use decisions, opting for the alternative that produces the most revenue.

general election Statewide election held on the first Tuesday after the first Monday of November in even-numbered years.

general-law city or county A city or county whose powers and structure of government are derived from state law.

general veto Gubernatorial power to reject an entire bill or budget; overruled only by an absolute two-thirds vote of both legislative houses.

governor California's highest-ranking executive officeholder; elected every 4 years.

grants-in-aid Payments from the national government to states to assist in fulfilling of public policy objectives.

incorporation Process by which residents of an urbanized area form a city.

independent expenditures Campaign spending by interest groups and political action committees on behalf of candidates.

initiative Progressive device by which people may put laws and constitutional amendments on the ballot after securing the required number of voters' signatures.

insurance commissioner Elected state executive who regulates the insurance industry; created by a 1988 initiative.

interest groups Nongovernmental organizations of individuals with similar concerns who seek to influence public policy.

item veto Gubernatorial power to delete or reduce the budget within a bill without rejecting the entire bill or budget; an absolute two-thirds vote of both houses of the state legislature is required to override.

Judicial Council Chaired by the chief justice of the state supreme court and composed of 21 judges and attorneys; makes the rules for court procedures, collects data on the courts' operations and workload, and gives seminars for judges.

legislative analyst Assistant to the legislature who studies the annual budget and proposed programs.

legislative committees Small groups of senators or assembly members who consider and make legislation in specialized areas, such as agriculture or education.

legislative counsel Assists the legislature in preparing bills and assessing their impact on existing legislation.

legislative initiatives Propositions placed on the ballot by the legislature rather than by initiative petition.

lieutenant governor Chief executive when the governor is absent from the state or disabled; succeeds the governor in case of death or other departure from office; casts a tie-breaking vote in the senate; is independently elected.

litigation Interest group tactic of challenging a law or policy in the courts to have it overruled, modified, or delayed.

lobbying Interest group efforts to influence political decision makers, often through paid professionals (lobbyists).

local agency formation commission (LAFCO) A county agency set up to oversee the creation and expansion of cities.

logrolling A give-and-take process in which legislators trade support for each other's bills.

mayor Ceremonial leader of a city, usually a position that alternates among council members, but in some large cities is directly elected and given substantial powers.

nonpartisan elections Progressive reform that removed party labels from ballots for local and judicial offices.

open primary Voters may support any listed candidate for an office irrespective of the voters' party affiliations; last considered in November 2004 when the voters rejected Proposition 62.

personal income tax A graduated tax on individual earnings adopted in 1935; the largest source of state revenues.

plea bargaining Reaching an agreement between the prosecution and the accused; the former gets a conviction, and the latter agrees to a reduced charge and lesser penalty.

political action committees (PACs) Mechanisms by which interest groups direct campaign contributions to preferred candidates.

Political Reform Act of 1974 Initiative requiring officials to disclose conflicts of interest, campaign contributions, and spending and requiring lobbyists to register.

preprimary endorsement Political parties' designation of preferred candidates in party primary elections, thus strengthening the role of party organizations in selecting candidates; banned by state law until 1990.

president pro tem Legislative leader of the state senate; chairs the senate Rules Committee; selected by the majority party.

primary election Election to choose party nominees; held in June of even-numbered years.

Progressives Members of an antimachine reform movement that reshaped the state's political institutions between 1907 and the 1920s.

property tax A tax on land and buildings; until the passage of Proposition 13 in 1978, the primary source of revenues for local governments.

Proposition 1A A 2004 ballot measure designed to prevent the state from taking revenues from local governments in times of fiscal stress.

Proposition 8 (Victims' Bill of Rights) A 1982 initiative that extended prison terms and thus increased California's prison population and expenditures.

Proposition 13 (Jarvis-Gann initiative) A 1978 ballot measure that cut property taxes.

Proposition 58 A 2004 proposition that set broad spending limits on state government and required the state to gradually set aside up to 3 percent of all revenues in a "rainy day" fund.

Proposition 98 A 1988 initiative awarding public education a fixed percentage of the state budget.

Proposition 140 A 1990 initiative limiting assembly members to three 2-year terms and senators and statewide elected officials to two 4-year terms and cutting the legislature's budget.

Proposition 172 A 1993 referendum in which voters made permanent a half-cent sales tax addition earmarked for local government expenditure on public safety.

Proposition 187 A 1994 initiative reducing government benefits for illegal immigrants; declared unconstitutional by federal courts in 1995.

Proposition 209 A 1996 initiative that eliminated affirmative action in California.

Proposition 227 A 1998 initiative limiting bilingual education to no more than one year.

public defender County officer representing defendants who cannot afford an attorney; appointed by the county board of supervisors.

public interest groups Organizations that purport to represent the general good rather than private interests.

reapportionment Adjustment of legislative district boundaries by the state legislature to keep all districts equal in population; done every 10 years after the national census.

recall Progressive reform allowing voters to remove elected officials by petition and majority vote.

redevelopment agencies Local government agencies operating within and controlled by cities to provide infrastructure and subsidies for new commercial and industrial developments in areas designated as "blighted" (usually old city centers and industrial areas).

referendum Progressive reform requiring the legislature to place certain measures before the voters, who may also repeal legislation by petitioning for a referendum.

Reynolds v. Sims A 1964 U.S. Supreme Court decision that ordered redistricting of the upper houses of all state legislatures by population instead of land area.

runoff election Election in which the top two candidates in a nonpartisan primary for trial court judge or local office face each other.

sales tax Statewide tax on most goods and products; adopted in 1933; local governments receive a portion of this tax.

school districts Local governments created by states to provide elementary and secondary education; governed by elected school boards.

secretary of state Elected state executive who keeps records and supervises elections.

Senate Rules Committee Chief committee for assigning chairs and committee appointments; chaired by the senate president pro tem.

Serrano v. Priest A 1972 California supreme court case that struck down the property tax as the main source of education funding.

Silicon Valley Top area for high-tech industries; located between San Jose and San Francisco.

single-issue groups Organized groups with unusually narrow policy objectives; not oriented toward compromise.

Southern Pacific Railroad Railroad company founded in 1861; developed a political machine that dominated state politics through the turn of the century.

speaker of the assembly Legislative leader of the assembly; selected by the majority party; controls committee appointments and the legislative process.

special districts Local government agencies providing a single service, such as fire protection or sewage disposal.

state auditor Assistant to the legislature who analyzes ongoing programs.

superintendent of public instruction Elected state executive in charge of public education.

superior courts Lower courts in which criminal and civil cases are first tried.

supreme court California's highest judicial body; hears appeals from lower courts.

term limits Limits on the number of terms that officeholders may serve; elected executive branch officers and state senators are limited to two 4-year terms, and assembly members are limited to three 2-year terms.

third parties Minor political parties that capture small percentages of the vote in the general election but are viewed as important protest vehicles.

"three strikes" A 1994 law and initiative requiring sentences of 25 years to life for anyone convicted of three felonies.

treasurer Elected state executive, responsible for state funds between collection and spending.

trial courts Lower courts in which civil and criminal cases are first tried.

user taxes Taxes on select commodities or services "used" by those who benefit directly from them.

veto See **general veto** and **item veto.**

Workingmen's party Denis Kearney's antirailroad, anti-Chinese organization; instrumental in rewriting California's constitution in 1879.

INDEX